THE POWER OF
GEMSTONES

This book is dedicated to the memory of my wife Bella, who
supported me during the years it took to compile these stories.

THIS IS A CARLTON BOOK

This edition published for Book Sales Inc.1996

Text copyright © Raymond J. L. Walters 1996
Design and artwork copyright © Carlton Books Limited 1996

ISBN 0-7858-0642-3

PROJECT EDITORS Ann Kay, Liz Wheeler
ART EDITOR Zoë Maggs
DESIGNER Rosamund Saunders
PRODUCTION Sarah Schuman

Printed and bound in Italy

THE POWER OF GEMSTONES

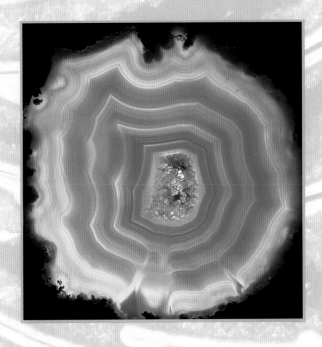

PRECIOUS AND SEMI-PRECIOUS STONES ♦ HEALING POWERS
MYTHICAL STONES ♦ SUPERSTITIONS, TALISMANS
AND MYSTICAL PROPERTIES

RAYMOND J.L. WALTERS

CHARTWELL
BOOKS, INC.

CONTENTS

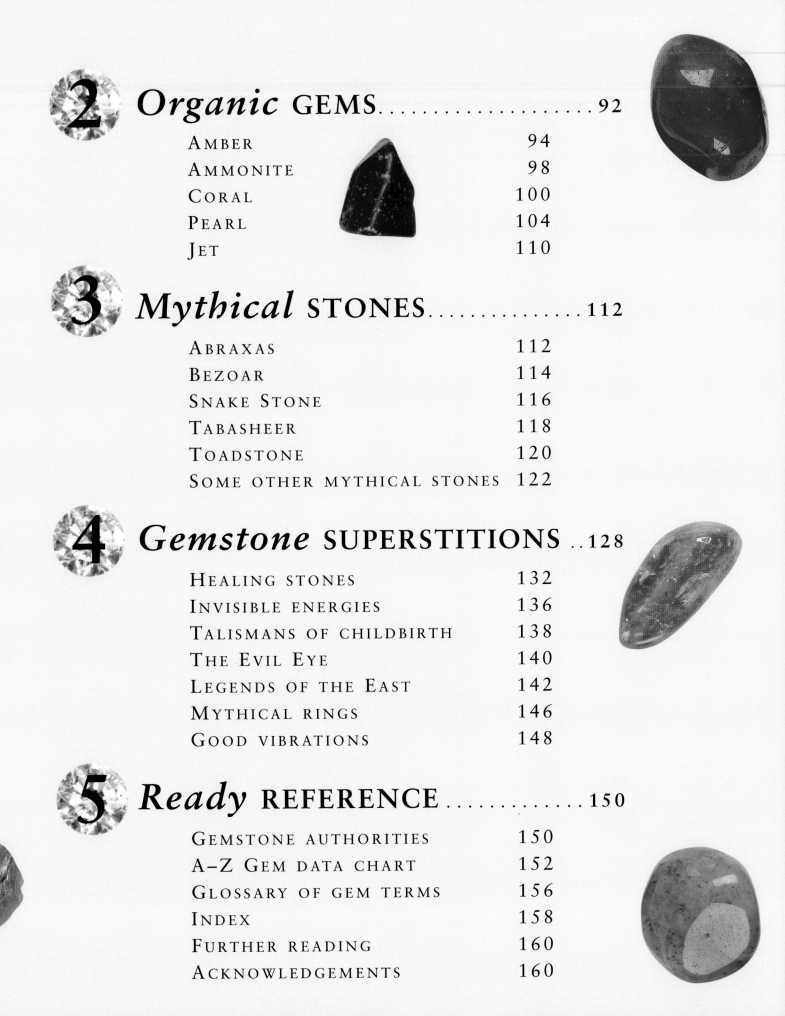

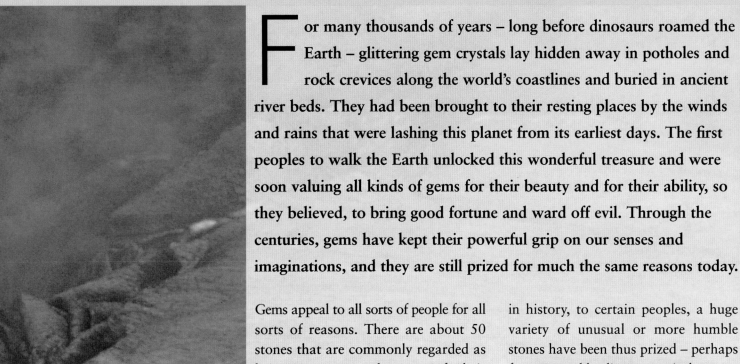

Introducing GEMS

For many thousands of years – long before dinosaurs roamed the Earth – glittering gem crystals lay hidden away in potholes and rock crevices along the world's coastlines and buried in ancient river beds. They had been brought to their resting places by the winds and rains that were lashing this planet from its earliest days. The first peoples to walk the Earth unlocked this wonderful treasure and were soon valuing all kinds of gems for their beauty and for their ability, so they believed, to bring good fortune and ward off evil. Through the centuries, gems have kept their powerful grip on our senses and imaginations, and they are still prized for much the same reasons today.

Gems appeal to all sorts of people for all sorts of reasons. There are about 50 stones that are commonly regarded as being gemstones, because of their beauty, colour, comparitive rarity, and durability.

However, there are many thousands of minerals and other hard substances found over the Earth, and many of these are just as entitled to the name gemstone – what is considered a gem is largely a matter of fashion. Most people think of the "top five" gems when they think of precious stones – ruby, sapphire, natural pearl, emerald and, of course, diamond – but a stone is as precious as people make it, and an ordinary piece of flint might be as valuable as a diamond to those who value its unique properties very highly. It is for this reason that you will find in this book all kinds of stones, including those you might be surprised to find in such a book. At certain times in history, to certain peoples, a huge variety of unusual or more humble stones have been thus prized – perhaps for supposed healing or magical powers rather than for their beauty – and, in this sense, have certainly been considered to be "gems".

Because a gem can really be any stone, everybody can own one, and they have been an important part of our history since the dawn of human life. In this book, we take you on a journey around all kinds of valued stones, giving mineralogical information and relating the many magical tales and legends that have become attached to them. You will also learn of all kinds of mythical stones that have cropped up time and time again ancient folklore. And, at the end of the book, you will find a useful ready-reference chart, providing basic data about those stones commonly accepted to be "gems".

In the beginning ...

If you own a gemstone, then you possess an antique as old as the universe itself. Going back to the very beginning... many millions of years ago, a gigantic, gaseous cloud of cosmic dust was slowly forming itself into the flaming star we call our Sun. A few more million years were to pass before our nine-planet solar system was born, each and every planet following its eternal elliptical orbit around the Sun.

Our planet was born around 50,000 million years ago, as a white-hot ball of gas. As this ball cooled slowly, all kinds of elements and compounds came into being. Lighter materials rose to the surface; heavier materials such as iron and nickel sank towards the central core – and gemstones were forming and growing.

WHERE ARE GEMSTONES FOUND?

The cooling Earth settled into three main layers: the outer crust, the semi-fluid mantle and the molten inner core. Most gemstones are made from minerals and so are found in the Earth's rocks, either on the surface or much further towards the heart of the planet. "Igneous" rocks, for example, are born within the mantle. This massive layer swirls with a substance called magma, which forms rock when it cools under the intense pressure found deep within the Earth. Solid rocks brought to the surface by the lava flowing from erupting volcanoes suggest that magma is made mainly of a substance known as peridotite, and the main minerals in peridotite are olivine and pyroxene.

By far the most prolific element in the Earth's crust is silicon. Silicon and

ABOVE: PATTERNS IN COOLED PAHOEHOE LAVA FROM THE HAWAIIAN VOLCANO KILAUEA IN 1974

BELOW: GEMSTONES HAVE BEEN FORMING THROUGHOUT THE ENTIRE HISTORY OF THIS PLANET

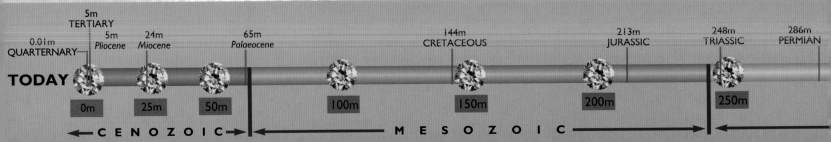

5m
TERTIARY
5m
Pliocene
24m
Miocene
65m
Palaeocene
144m
CRETACEOUS
213m
JURASSIC
248m
TRIASSIC
286m
PERMIAN

0.01m
QUARTERNARY

TODAY

0m   25m   50m   100m   150m   200m   250m

← CENOZOIC → ← MESOZOIC →

FACT & FANTASY

ACCORDING TO THE ANCIENTS, EVERY PRECIOUS STONE HAD A PARTICULAR TALISMANIC POWER OVER THE FORCES OF DARKNESS – FROM EMERALDS AND DIAMONDS, THROUGH SEMI-PRECIOUS GEMS SUCH AS GARNET AND MALACHITE, TO MORE MUNDANE STONES SUCH AS FLINT. BETWEEN THEM, GEMS COULD OVERCOME WITCHES, WIZARDS, AND THE HAGS THAT WERE SAID TO RIDE HORSES AND CATTLE ROUGHSHOD OVER THE COUNTRYSIDE IN THE DEAD OF NIGHT.

oxygen combine easily and quickly to form silicon dioxide, and the majority of mineral compounds contain these elements in varying proportion. Next time you stroll along a golden, sandy beach, anywhere in the world, remind yourself that the surface beneath your feet is actually made of tiny grains of silicon dioxide, otherwise known as quartz, stained golden by the soluble iron carried to it by sea-water.

All kinds of gemstones are excellent examples of silicon compounds, most of them containing silicon and oxygen. They also contain various other related elements, which produce varying proportions of colour.

THE HUMAN ELEMENT

When early humans first discovered gem crystals, they noticed how different they were from most other stones and rocks – they had attractive colours and pleasing,

uniform shapes. Because they were very hard, little was done with these gems at first, except for binding them with animal or vegetable sinews and wearing them as ornaments. Soon, however, these first peoples discovered how to chip and cleave these stones and used many of them as tools and weapons.

And when they looked deeply into the hearts of some of the crystals they found, they were awed by a strange sense of power that so many of these gems seemed to possess. Early man would set aside an extraordinarily beautiful gem crystal and venerate it as the talisman of his household, looking to the gem to protect his family from harm and guide his spears and arrows to their targets on hunting trips.

ANCIENT WISDOM

Crystals and gemstones were also venerated by the ancients, and they too believed that these beautiful, cold, hard stones must be endowed with supernatural powers that would protect them from illness, misfortune and danger. Travellers and pilgrims regularly carried gemstone talismans to keep them safe from harm – even on short visits to the next village.

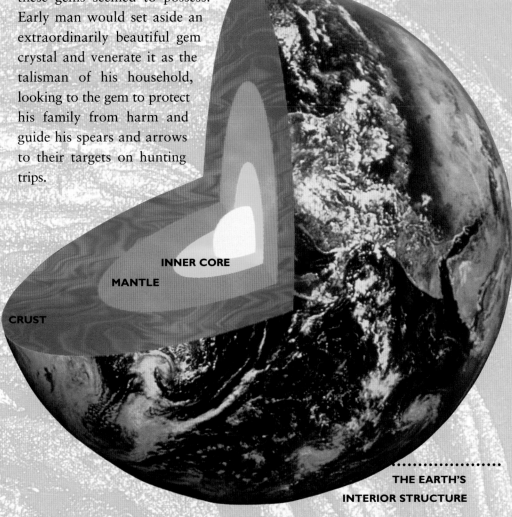

INNER CORE

MANTLE

CRUST

THE EARTH'S INTERIOR STRUCTURE

| 360m CARBONIFEROUS | 408m DEVONIAN | 438m SILURIAN | 505m ORDOVICIAN | 590m CAMBRIAN |

| 300m | 350m | 400m | 450m | 500m | 550m | 600m |

P A L A E O Z O I C

What are GEMS?

As we've seen, the term gemstone can be used extremely loosely, but gemmologists obviously work within much more precise guidelines. The science of gemmology divides gems into two different kinds: inorganic and organic. In this book, the two main chapters are devoted to these two categories.

• Inorganic: These are hard, naturally occurring minerals with a regular chemical structure. The majority of gemstones are inorganic, and of the thousands of minerals extracted from the interior of this planet, only about twenty are given the supreme accolade of gemstone – for their rarity, beauty, durability and hardness.

• Organic: These come from either animals or plants – for example, amber, which comes from fossilized tree resin, and pearls, produced by shellfish. Other examples include coral, jet and tortoiseshell, while for centuries the bones and teeth of large land and marine animals were carved or engraved and used as ornamental brooches, necklaces and statuettes.

A WEIGHTY MATTER

Both inorganic and organic gems are weighed in units known as carats, and one carat is one-fifth of a gram. (The carat is also used to describe how pure gold is.) Various tales are told of the origins of this term, and the following is distilled from a huge collection of writings on the magical, spiritual and medical properties of gemstones and metals.

There is a tree, known as the carob tree, which grows in the East and in many countries bordering the Mediterranean. It is well suited for growth in arid areas because its roots drive down deeply in the search for water. The fruits of this tree are leathery looking, darkish brown pods some 30 cm long and shaped like giant runner beans. In the fresh pods are many small black seeds, and between each seed is a sweet syrupy liquid, looking and tasting like honey. Drying and finely grinding the pods produces a powder – resembling in texture a sweetened cocoa powder – that is used in the manufacture and preparation of chocolate-style bars, drinks and sweets.

EASTERN WISDOM

For thousands of years, gem-traders all over the East have used the tiny black seeds of the carob tree bean to weigh their gemstones. The average weight of a single

FACT & FANTASY

IN 16TH-CENTURY ENGLAND, THE "GRAIN" WEIGHT WAS USED TO WEIGH PRECIOUS STONES. A CONTEMPORARY CHRONICLER NOTED: "THE LEAST PORTION OF WEIGHT IN USE IS THE GRAYNE, MEANING A GRAYNE OF WHEAT, DRIED AND GATHERED OUT OF THE MIDDLE EAR". BECAUSE THE WEIGHTS BECAME INCONSISTENT AS THE WHEAT GRAINS DRIED, THIS SYSTEM WAS ABANDONED, ALTHOUGH THE NAME LIVES ON WITH PRESENT-DAY DIAMOND DEALERS. THEY STILL REFER TO A 1-CARAT STONE AS A FOUR-GRAINER, 0.75 CARATS AS A THREE-GRAINER AND A HALF-CARAT STONE AS A TWO-GRAINER.

carob bean seed is marginally short of the modern metric carat and the derivation of the word "carob" and "carat" are almost certainly very closely linked.

With the improving accuracy of weighing scales, it became the practice to weigh gemstones in milligrams, but the discrepancies in the weights used by different dealers, some clinging to the old methods, caused certain carats to weigh

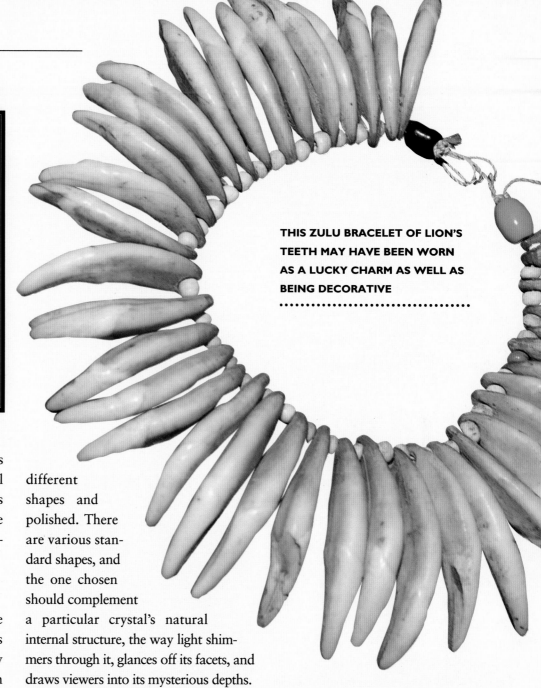

THIS ZULU BRACELET OF LION'S TEETH MAY HAVE BEEN WORN AS A LUCKY CHARM AS WELL AS BEING DECORATIVE

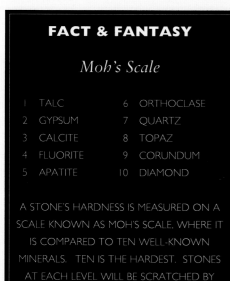

as little as 190 mg and others as much as 215 mg. Finally, the International Committee on Weights and Measures agreed that 200 mg should represent the metric carat, and this was adopted internationally between 1908 and 1930.

MOH'S SCALE

Yet another system is used to measure the hardness of inorganic gems – gems must be tough if they are to be worn day after day as jewellery – and the system used is called Moh's Scale, after the German mineralogist Friedrich Mohs. The scale runs from 1 to 10, with 10 being the hardest, and is based on how resistant the gem in question is to being scratched.

All inorganic gems are crystalline, with a fixed, geometric structure. Some are found as rough crystals, whereas others may have been turned into smooth pebbles as rivers or streams tumbled over their surface. To be used in jewellery, many gems are cut into different shapes and polished. There are various standard shapes, and the one chosen should complement a particular crystal's natural internal structure, the way light shimmers through it, glances off its facets, and draws viewers into its mysterious depths.

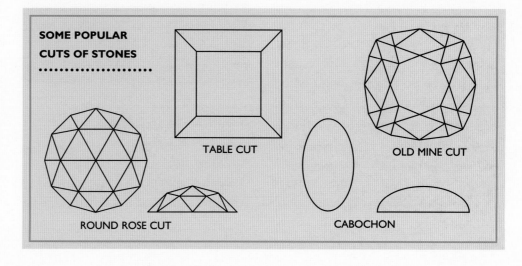

SOME POPULAR CUTS OF STONES

ROUND ROSE CUT

TABLE CUT

OLD MINE CUT

CABOCHON

False GEMSTONES

Before the advent of the Verneuil furnace (see corundum, below), imitation gems were made of glass-like materials, or "paste", coloured with various substances. For example, cobalt gives a blue colour and yellow is produced by adding silver salts or titanium compounds. These colourings give a greater brilliance and density to the glass, but also make it a little softer, with a different refractive index (the way in which a stone distorts light that passes through it).

A CLOSE MATCH

Man-made synthetic gemstones are fully crystalline and differ only marginally from the natural minerals that they imitate. Synthetics must be cheaper than the genuine article and must be produced from crystals large enough for the lapidary (cutter and polisher of stones) to work with them effectively. It should also be possible to provide sufficient quantities of stones to justify the cost of producing them in the first place.

Under the microscope, many synthetic gems contain tiny bubbles, and there will be no natural "inclusions" (such as marks, small cavities filled with either liquid or gas, or particles of other minerals). Moulded glass "stones" may show mould marks around the girdle of the stone and the edges of the facets will tend to be rounded rather than sharp, unless the imitation has been re-cut.

FACT & FANTASY

"COMPOSITE" STONES ARE MADE BY JOINING TOGETHER TWO OR MORE PIECES OF DIFFERENT PRECIOUS MINERALS – A TECHNIQUE KNOWN SINCE ROMAN TIMES. FOR EXAMPLE, THREE PIECES OF WHITE JADE HAVE BEEN JOINED TOGETHER WITH A GREEN CEMENT TO GIVE THE APPEARANCE OF VALUABLE "IMPERIAL" JADE. THERE MAY BE A GOOD REASON FOR PRODUCING A COMPOSITE STONE, SUCH AS COVERING A SOFT MINERAL LIKE OPAL WITH A HARD, PROTECTIVE LAYER OF QUARTZ.

SOME NOTABLE EXAMPLES

• *Diamond*
Diamonds are a form of carbon, and so synthetic stones are made from submitting carbon or graphite to very high temperatures and extreme pressure.

• *Corundum*
Corundum is a mineral that includes sapphires and rubies. It was not until around 1900 that the French chemist August Verneuil developed a special furnace that could produce corundum in large enough pieces to make synthetic gems. This was done by fusing granules of powdered aluminium oxide (alumina) with a very hot flame. As it cools, this melted powder forms a large crystal called a boule, which is effectively a single crystal with the same physical and optical attributes as natural corundum, although it also has a vertical line of weakness that often causes it to split in two. These boules are produced in many different colours by adding metal oxides to the alumina powder; chromic oxide produces synthetic ruby, while the addition of titanium and iron oxides produces synthetic sapphire.

• *Emerald*
Crystals of aluminium beryllium silicate (emerald) of good colour and quality have been grown in the laboratory using either the "hydrothermal pressure bomb" or "flux melt" methods. The hydrothermal method depends on the fact that, under great pressure, water boils at temperatures far higher than 100°C. At these temperatures, water can dissolve silicates to form a saturated solution. On cooling, its constituents

come out of solution and form crystals. The flux melt method is fundamentally the same, except that the basic material that forms the emerald material is dissolved in boron and lead oxide and held at 1300°C for about seven days before being allowed to cool naturally to room temperature.

Other methods include growing a "skin" over an existing cut emerald. A good gemmologist, however, will be able to detect any synthetic emerald.

1

Inorganic GEMS

"Like everything else created by Mother Nature, this mineral world looks comparatively simple until we begin to investigate its real character – which turns out to be enormously complex. The precise mechanisms of crystal formation are not yet fully understood. We do know, however, that all life on this earth is dependent on those mineral substances that make up the planet's crust and, in the process, sometimes produce those 'flowers of the underworld' that have always delighted the human eye and stimulated the human imagination."

FROM *THE BOOK OF SACRED STONES:*
FACT AND FALLACY IN THE CRYSTAL WORLD,
BY BARBARA G. WALKER

As we have already mentioned, all of the inorganic gems are made from minerals, from the countless different kinds of rocks that are found across the world. Gem minerals have a crystalline structure, and it is this that gives them the majority of their very special properties. You can find out much more about crystal structure on pages 16 and 17.

In this first chapter you will find detailed examples of all sorts of inorganic stones that people have valued down the centuries for their beauty or sacred power – from the brilliant diamond to rather more humble materials such as flint.

The stones that are featured in this chapter have been arranged according to colour, following the spectrum of natural light. First come the red and orange stones, followed by the yellow, green, blue, and violet ones. Those that vary widely in colour are dealt with next, and the whole sequence ends with the white and colourless gems, as it is all the colours of the spectrum that make up white light.

Remember that most gems come in a wide range of different colours, not just the ones that have been featured here.

CRYSTALS

"Crystal is found in those high places where the winter snows have gathered in great quantity, and it is surely ice."

PLINY, IN HISTORIA NATURALIS

Any crystalline material has a fixed internal structure made up of lots of regularly arranged atoms. The structure of crystals is of prime importance to the gemmologist, a major physical characteristic that enables him to tell similar gems apart and to distinguish genuine gemstones from any kind of imitation. Crystal formation is vital to all kinds of other disciplines too, and the roots of gemmology spread widely across mineralogy, chemistry, physics and geology.

Mineralogy developed and gained its status during the nineteenth century, while gemmology has developed as an even newer scientific discipline within the last six or seven decades, as a means of detecting synthetic or imitation stones, as well as those that have been altered in some way – by staining, heat, nuclear radiation, filling in of cavities and so on.

FROZEN ICE

What is a crystal, then, and where did the name come from? It was actually the ancient Greeks who first gave the name *crystallos* to transparent quartz – which is also known as rock crystal (see pages 20-21). The word *crystallos* literally translated means "frozen ice". During antiquity, quartz crystals were believed to have been formed by the action of intense cold on the still waters found in remote mountain caverns, over long periods of time.

By the 1770s, the long-held ice crystal theory had been rejected and was being replaced by the idea that crystals grew by the addition of new layers, the particles of which emerged from a solution. Gradually, over the years, this has been developed into a set of physical laws, one of which states:

"When measured at the same temperature, all crystals of the same substance have the same angles between corresponding faces."

FORTUNATE MISHAPS

A certain man named René-Just Haüy, a botanist working around the turn of the nineteenth century, made an important discovery when he accidentally dropped and broke a large calcite crystal. It shattered into hundreds of fragments. When Haüy studied these fragments, he noticed something curious: all the pieces had identical shapes, no matter how minute the fragments, and from this observation he arrived at a most important conclusion – that a crystal is built up from a large number of very small units, all with the same shape. He gave these units the name "integrant molecules". What we now know is that the outward shape of a crystal reflects its internal structure, which, as we said earlier, consists of atoms arranged in a regular, lattice-like pattern.

Building on Haüy's idea of a "crystal house" constructed from many bricks, another scientist called Bravais calculated that the lattice structures could be grouped as seven main crystal systems. These depended on whether the relative lengths of the three axes of a crystal are at right angles or inclined to each other, and in what proportion and what angle of inclination. These systems are:

1. Cubic.
2. Tetragonal.
3. Trigonal.
4. Hexagonal.
5. Orthorhombic.
6. Monoclinic.
7. Triclinic.

AN ORDERLY AFFAIR

Further proof of the structure of crystals was presented in 1912, when an experiment undertaken by Max von Laue showed how X-rays passing through a crystal were scattered in a regular and distinctive pattern for each and every mineral. This work was further investigated and expanded into the science of crystallography by W. H. Bragg, in 1913. His son, W. L. Bragg, continued his father's important work.

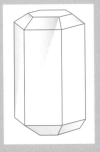

HEXAGONAL
Four axes produce six-sided shapes. There are three equal axes that intersect at 60 ° and a fourth axis perpendicular to the others

ORTHOROMBIC
Three unequal axes at right angles to each other, producing unusual shapes such as variations on the pyramid form

TETRAGONAL
Three axes, of which two are equal, at right angles to each other, gives shapes such as four- or eight-sided pyramids or prisms

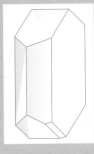

MONOCLINIC
Three unequal axes, two of which intersect at an oblique angle. Gives, for example, prism-like shapes

CUBIC
Three axes of the same length, at right angles to each other

TRICLINIC
Three unequal axes, all obliquely angled. The shapes of these crystals have far less symmetry than the other six systems

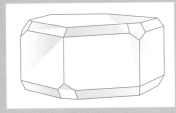

TRIGONAL
Similar to hexagonal

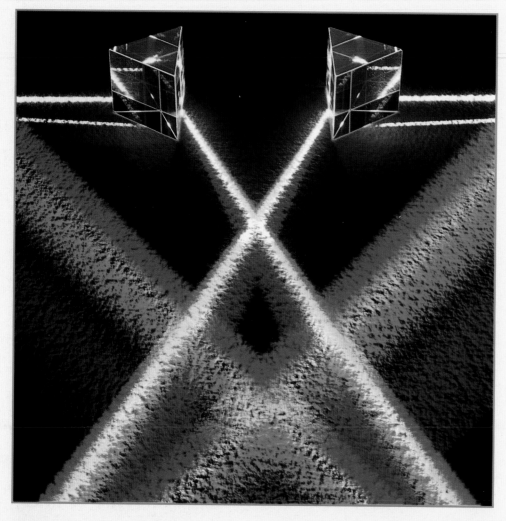

exhibits piezoelectricity when the crystal is placed under stress, and for this reason is found in instruments for detecting depth and pressure under water.

AN INNER WORLD

Anyone looking into the heart of some crystals, under a microscope, will be astounded by another important feature – inclusions. This term is used for anything that is trapped inside a stone, from a cavity to a fragment of another mineral, and includes minute, beautifully shaped crystals, feathery cracks, bubbles in all shapes and sizes, perhaps filled with fluid or gas, and traces of plant or animal matter. For example, "horse tails" and "sunbursts" of byssolite asbestos fibres characterize a certain type of green garnet.

The various types of inclusion arise for different reasons:

1. They were in the vicinity before the host crystal formed and are usually other solid crystals or earthy matter.

2. They may be droplets of the "liquor" that gave rise to the host crystal and/or other crystals that have formed and grown at the same time.

3. They were formed later than the host crystal, such as cracks into which mineral-rich liquid has percolated and formed minute crystals.

FORMING CLOSE BONDS

At the time a crystal is being formed, the atoms of all its constituent chemicals are rushing about at fantastic speeds. It is the forces of attraction known as atomic bonds that bring them together to form an orderly pattern. This is rather like shaking a box of table-tennis balls and watching them settle into a geometric stacking pattern.

One important consequence of this regular formation, which is based on symmetrical and asymmetrical planes, is that certain properties will vary with direction. For example, kyanite crystals

have a hardness of 7 across their width and 5 along their length.

Some stones have electrical properties under certain conditions:

• Quartz (rock crystal) is piezoelectric. When it is subjected to mechanical stress, quartz develops an electrical charge on its surfaces, making it ideal for use in gas lighters.

• Tourmaline is pyroelectric, which simply means that it develops an electrical charge when heated. This makes it a good material to use in thermometers. Tourmaline also

SEEING THE LIGHT

A crystal's optical properties are a major part of the magic and power of gems. A ray of light entering any crystal is slowed down and "refracted" (bent). Here, once again, the structure comes into play. For any crystal except those belonging to the cubic system, light entering the crystal is immediately split into two rays, which travel through the crystal at different speeds and are refracted by different amounts. The refractive index (RI) measures how far light is bent by a crystal and is just one of the ways that gemmologists can determine whether a gemstone is genuine or not.

••••••••••••••••••••••••••••••••••••

EMBEDDED RUBIES PHOTOGRAPHED IN ULTRAVIOLET LIGHT

GLOWING IN THE DARK

Certain gems, when exposed to the short, invisible wavelengths of ultraviolet light or X-rays, absorb the energy of these rays and then emit that same energy in longer, visible wavelengths. Ruby and emerald, for example, will glow like red-hot coals, while diamond is seen to emit an eerie bluish light. This strange phenomenon is called fluorescence, after the mineral – fluorite – in which it was first studied. A colour photograph of the fluorescing pattern of a particular piece of jewellery can provide a valuable identity document for insurance purposes, should the piece be lost or stolen.

Some gemstones delay the emission of these changed wavelengths, which in turn causes the gem to glow in the dark even after the shorter rays have been totally removed. This afterglow is known as phosphorescence. The phosphorescent afterglow of diamond is a particularly good identification mark.

MOVING ON

The remainder of this first chapter is devoted to the various fascinating facts and fantasies surrounding a broad selection of inorganic gems, arranged according to the colours of the spectrum. So, read on...

FACT & FANTASY

SOME INCLUSIONS ARE VISIBLE WITH THE NAKED EYE, BUT WITH A MICROSCOPE, GEMMOLOGISTS CAN USE ALL KINDS OF MINUTE INCLUSIONS AS VALUABLE IDENTIFICATION AIDS. THEY REVEAL NOT JUST THE IDENTITY OF THE GEM AND WHERE IN THE WORLD IT CAME FROM, BUT IN SOME CASES PINPOINT THE VERY MINE FROM WHICH IT WAS RECOVERED. FOR EXAMPLE, TINY ACTINOLITE INCLUSIONS IN EMERALD SUGGEST THAT IT WAS POSSIBLY MINED IN RUSSIA AND NOT IN COLOMBIA, WHILE EMERALDS FROM THE COLOMBIAN CHIVOR MINE OFTEN CONTAIN CRYSTALS OF PYRITES, CALCITE RHOMBS AND "THREE-PHASE INCLUSIONS" – IRREGULARLY SHAPED CAVITIES FILLED WITH A LIQUID THAT CONTAINS A BUBBLE OF GAS AND A HALITE CRYSTAL. INCLUSIONS ARE A GOOD SIGN OF A GENUINE STONE, AND GEMSTONES DESIGNATED AS FLAWLESS ARE THOSE IN WHICH INCLUSIONS CAN ONLY BE SEEN WITH A VERY HIGH-POWERED MICROSCOPE.

SPINEL

"The stones are dug on the King's account and no one else dares dig for them on pain of death as well as seizure of worldly possessions, nor may any take the gems out of the kingdom"

MARCO POLO (1254–1324)

Spinel comes in various different colours, but red spinel is the most popular. Belonging to the cubic system, spinel is magnesium aluminate, and the red colour comes from chromium and iron deposits. For many years, red spinel was thought to be a kind of ruby known as Balas Ruby, and the ancients classified this stone as a female ruby. Most "rubies" brought home as plunder by the Crusaders on their return from the Holy Wars during the Middle Ages are easily identified as spinels by qualified gemmologists.

Marco Polo's writings show just how revered the Balas Ruby was in the Orient. He writes:

"In the province [Badachschan], those fine and valuable gems the Balas Rubies are found. They are got in certain rocks among the mountains and in the search for them the people dig great caves beneath the earth just as it is by miners for silver. There is but one special mountain that produces them and it is called Syghinan. The King collects them all and sends them to other kings as presents. He also acts to keep the Balas at great value for if he allowed all persons to mine for them the world would be filled with them and they would be valueless."

THE BLACK PRINCE'S RUBY

During the fourteenth century, the king of Castille, in Spain, defeated Abu Said, Moorish king of Granada, in battle. Abu Said journeyed to Castille to negotiate terms and plead for mercy.

Now Abu Said carried with him many jewels, among which were four huge Balas rubies, which he anxiously kept out of sight. Peter welcomed Abu Said amiably and extended an invitation to a banquet prepared in his honour.

However, treachery prevailed. Peter – given the name Peter the Cruel because of his harsh abuse of power – had given specific instructions that all the servants of the Moorish king were to be slain during the feast. Peter himself murdered his kingly guest with a dagger, and stole the treasured Balas rubies.

Several years later, Henry of Trastamara (Peter's half brother) rebelled and attacked Castille, forcing Peter to flee. But Peter had formed an alliance with Edward, the Black Prince of England, upon whom he called for assistance. Together, in 1367, they succeeded in defeating Henry of Trastamara.

THE *History* OF RED SPINEL

By way of thanks for this valuable assistance, Peter presented the Black Prince with the largest of the four Balas rubies that had been stolen from the king of Granada.

CROWN JEWELS OF ENGLAND

The great ruby presented to the Black Prince now occupies an important place in the collection of the English Crown Jewels. At one time, this gleaming red stone was seen fixed to the helmet of Henry V, as he fought at the battle of Agincourt in 1415. At the battle of Bosworth, this great Balas ruby was worn prominently on the helmet of Richard III.

During Cromwell's puritanical dictatorship, in the 1600s, the English Crown jewels were broken up and destroyed. The gold that formed the crown was melted and reformed into coins and various other artefacts; the jewels were dispersed among whoever would buy them. However, fate determined that the jeweller who had purchased the great ruby was to resell it to Charles II shortly after the restoration of the English monarchy, in 1660.

THE BRITISH IMPERIAL STATE CROWN

This great Balas ruby is now set into the British Imperial State Crown. It is approximately five centimetres long, weighs about 150 carats and is like a distorted octahedron (two pyramids placed base to base). At some point, a hole has been drilled right through the

THE Legends ◆ OF RED SPINEL

stone, from the apex to the base.

At each end of the stone, two smaller holes have been drilled at right angles to the first, perpendicular hole, possibly so that it could be fixed to a helmet. At some later date, one of the smaller pierced holes at the top of the stone has been filled in with a small genuine ruby.

PROTECTION FROM HARM

According to traditional folklore, the Balas Ruby confers upon its owner exactly the same benefits as those provided by genuine rubies.

It is said to afford protection from disaster – both physical and financial – with additional powers to enlarge the mind, control thoughts and expand the imagination.

For these supposed properties, red spinel is the gemstone recommended to be worn by doctors, nurses and all those engaged in the medical profession.

THE BRITISH IMPERIAL STATE CROWN SET WITH THE GREAT BALAS RUBY

GARNET

"...to resist melancholy and poison, stop the spitting of blood and dissolve tartar in the body"

WILLIAM ROWLAND, PHYSICIAN, ON A SPECIAL
MEDICINE PREPARED FROM GARNETS, 1669

Many chemical forms of garnet exist, but at the present time only six are recognized as being of gem quality. These are: pyrope, almandine, spessartine, grossular, andradite and uvarovite. Garnet shapes belong to the cubic system and are usually found as rhombic dodecahedra (with 12 lozenge-shaped faces) or icositetrahedra (24 trapezium-shaped faces) or a combination of these, depending on the chemical composition of the stone.

Garnet is the stone associated with birth and the month of January. It is also noted for its toughness. When garnets are cut *en cabachon*, that is, flat on the bottom, they are called carbuncles. Larger crystals of garnet have been uncovered when mining for various other minerals, while they are also found in river-bed potholes containing alluvial deposits, inside pot-holes in flash flood courses, and buried in dry river beds.

SHADES AND HUES

Colour varieties occur in all kinds of different shades, ranging from colour-less to red; violet to orange; yellow to green; and brown to black, although the majority of people think of garnets as being red.

During the early days of digging for diamonds in South Africa, miners sold the red garnets that they found as "Cape Rubies". Colour variation in garnet is determined by elements that enter the crystal lattice by a natural process during the time in which the crystal is forming.

ANCIENT BEAUTY

Beautiful, fiery red pyrope garnets recovered from the ancient mines of Bohemia are often seen set in antique jewellery, while almandine garnet has

THE RED GARNET CRYSTAL, ABOVE, IS
SET IN AN OCTAGONAL STEP-CUT
DIAMOND
••

an attractive red-purple hue, depending on its iron content.

Spessartite garnets range from yellow to brown and orange to flame red. The massive green variety, which may contain up to five per cent water, is called hydro-grossular garnet and can be as large as a boulder, or even as a hill. This is also called Transvaal Jade, although it resembles jade only in colour. Beads and figurines are frequently carved from hydro-grossular garnet, and lately this material has been found in pink to rose-red colorations. Despite being found in such a wide variety of colours there is, strangely, just one colour that never graces a garnet: blue.

HESSONITE

A type of grossular garnet called hessonite, which comes mostly from Sri Lanka, Switzerland and South Africa, provides attractive reddish orange and brownish yellow stones. Sri Lanka provides not only hessonite and many other forms of garnet, it is an

island rich in rocks and minerals used for industrial purposes; it is the world's largest producer of graphite, a form of carbon with many uses but most commonly known for its contribution to pencil lead. Long known as the land of gems, Sri Lanka has 44 varieties of precious and semiprecious gemstones.

GARNETS COME IN A RAINBOW VARIETY OF HUES, ALTHOUGH MANY PEOPLE THINK OF GARNETS AS BEING RED IN COLOUR. BELOW ARE A UVAROVITE CRYSTAL (CENTRE), AND GREEN, ORANGE AND COLOURLESS GARNET CRYSTALS
....

THE *Legends* ◆ OF GARNET

THE WARRIOR'S TALISMAN

Since earliest times, gems have been valued as talismans that will keep their wearers safe from harm, which is why children in parts of Greece still carry garnet talismans to guard them against drowning. In particular, warriors and soldiers from all over the world have placed their destinies in the hands of garnet stones, trusting that they will not only guard against injury and death and bring victory, but that they will also guarantee the peace and tranquillity needed to enjoy it.

Legendary belief in this talisman of war prompted many Crusaders to carry a red garnet somewhere about their person, and their jewellers were instructed to set the stone into signet rings, belt buckles, sword hilts and shields. In common with many other red stones, garnet was also believed to have a magical power that staunched the flow of blood, and so surgeons would place the stone on or near serious wounds and haemorrhages. Even today, fighting men from the Middle East and Asia are more than likely to carry a talisman of red garnet into battle.

Linked with the ancient belief that garnet is able to staunch blood-flow, is a superstition that it also has the power to inflict mortal wounds. During a rebellion of Indian nationalists, in

1892, British troops were ambushed and fired on by Hanza tribesmen concealed in well-positioned hiding places along the borders of Kashmir. Interspersed with the volleys of lead balls from the Hanza's ancient, muzzle-loading guns were ball-shaped garnets, which caused many serious and often fatal wounds to the British "Red Coats".

HEALING GARNET

According to the eminent William Rowland esq., doctor of Physic during the 1600s, medicine prepared from a "magistery" of red garnet was prescribed by him to stimulate the heart, reduce its palpitations, improve blood

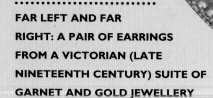

....
FAR LEFT AND FAR RIGHT: A PAIR OF EARRINGS FROM A VICTORIAN (LATE NINETEENTH CENTURY) SUITE OF GARNET AND GOLD JEWELLERY

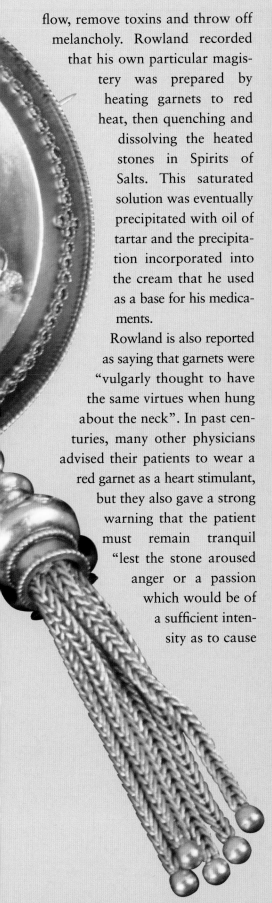

flow, remove toxins and throw off melancholy. Rowland recorded that his own particular magistery was prepared by heating garnets to red heat, then quenching and dissolving the heated stones in Spirits of Salts. This saturated solution was eventually precipitated with oil of tartar and the precipitation incorporated into the cream that he used as a base for his medicaments.

Rowland is also reported as saying that garnets were "vulgarly thought to have the same virtues when hung about the neck". In past centuries, many other physicians advised their patients to wear a red garnet as a heart stimulant, but they also gave a strong warning that the patient must remain tranquil "lest the stone aroused anger or a passion which would be of a sufficient intensity as to cause

FACT & FANTASY

SKYSCRAPERS BUILT ON NEW YORK'S MANHATTAN ISLAND HAVE DEEP FOUNDATIONS DRIVEN INTO THE ISLAND'S BEDROCK, WHICH CONTAINS A VAST AMOUNT OF GARNET. GREAT PRESSURE EXERTED BY THE MASS OF THE ISLAND HAS CAUSED THE GARNET TO BE RECONSTITUTED OR REFORMED AS SMALL AND OFTEN MISSHAPEN STONES, MOST OF WHICH ARE NOT OF GEM QUALITY.

apoplexy". Physicians recommending the wearing of garnet jewellery as a cure for melancholia also gave a warning – that the sadness would be exchanged for insomnia.

THE STONE OF LIGHT

According to some records, a large garnet carbuncle was set upon a pedestal in the centre of Noah's Ark. Legend describes a bright light that poured from the carbuncle, causing the whole of the ship to be illuminated by day as well as by night.

Early Spanish astrologers showed garnet on their charts as representing the Sun, while the Koran teaches its adherents that a carbuncle illuminates the fourth heaven.

Given as a gift, garnet is said to confer upon its new owner the dual gifts of loyalty and constant affection, but warnings have always been given to those who own and wear garnet. It is said that, when the stone begins to lose its lustre, this is the herald of imminent danger and disaster. Folklore also has it that, for the business man, garnet of any colour encourages success, especially if the garnet is the green demantoid. And for those who dream of garnet... a solution to a mystery is soon to be revealed.

CENTRE: A DIAMOND AND GARNET MOUNTED REVERSE CRYSTAL INTAGLIO BROOCH, POSSIBLY LATE NINETEENTH CENTURY

RUBY

"Some asked me where the rubies grew;

And nothing did I say,

But with my finger pointed to

The lips of Julia.

Some ask'd how Pearls do grow, and where?

Then spake I to my girl –

To "part her lips"; and show'd them there

The quarrelets of Pearl."

ROBERT HERRICK,
POET (1591-1674)

MASCULINE AND FEMININE STONES

Along with many other gems, rubies were divided into male and female stones by ancient writers. The extraordinary theory that gemstones could be sexed was first advanced by the ancient Greek philosopher and naturalist Theophrastus, and this theory came to be accepted and taught for hundreds of years in Greece, Europe, and much of Northern Africa.

The Roman writer Pliny continued to expound this theory. He wrote: "Furthermore, in each variety there are

R uby is a type of corundum, or aluminium oxide, and its trigonal crystals are found as six-sided prisms. Pure corundum is colourless; the red colour of ruby comes from the presence of chromium, which is also responsible for making rubies fluoresce like glowing coals under ultra-violet light. At times, a minute amount of iron will be present in the crystal lattice, giving a slight brownish tint to the stone and masking the fluorescence to some extent.

The kinds of inclusions seen in the stones – such as needles of rutile, zircon crystals, liquid-filled cavities and so on – are important in that they help to distinguish natural stones from man-made, synthetic ones.

The finest-quality rubies are mined in the Mogok region of Burma, where the colour is compared to that of pigeon's blood. In Thailand, small traces of iron give the rubies an almost indiscernible brownish tint, while stones from Sri Lanka are more pink than red. The palest pink gemstones are generally known as pink sapphires.

THE Legends
◆ OF RUBY

so-called "male" and "female" stones, of which the former are the more brilliant, while the latter have a weaker lustre." He goes on to tell us that the counterfeiters were as busy then as now: "The duller stones, it is said, when steeped in vinegar for fourteen days, shine with a lustre that persists for as many months. They are also counterfeited in glass."

STONE OF FIRE

Pliny did not separate red stones into different types. All red stones, such as rubies, red garnets and red spinel are referred to as "carbunculii", although his remark that these stones are unaffected by fire seems to apply only to rubies. Epiphanius, sometime bishop of Seville, whose books were standard texts for students of medicine, also took up the theme of heat and fire. He advised that rubies generated such a great heat when cast into water that they caused the water to boil, and commented that the "inextinguishable fire that glowed

within the ruby could not be hidden; it would shine through any cloth or other material that was wrapped round it".

The Elizabethans were similarly impressed by this stone. Sir Jerome Horsey, trusted messenger of Queen Elizabeth I of England, was sent on one occasion on a diplomatic visit to Ivan the Terrible of Russia. Sir Jerome noted Ivan's comments on the virtues of ruby: "Oh! this is the most comfortable to the hart, brain, vigar, and memorie of man. It clarifies conjelled and corrupt bloud."

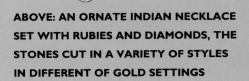

ABOVE: AN ORNATE INDIAN NECKLACE SET WITH RUBIES AND DIAMONDS, THE STONES CUT IN A VARIETY OF STYLES IN DIFFERENT OF GOLD SETTINGS

....

FACT & FANTASY

ONE IN A LONG LIST OF TITLES CONFERRED ON PAST KINGS OF BURMA WAS "LORD OF THE RUBIES". WHEN THE ROYAL MINERS REPORTED THE FIND OF A SIGNIFICANT RUBY, IT BECAME THE KING'S CUSTOM TO DISPATCH A PROCESSION OF NOBLES TO THE MINES. THE PROCESSION WAS ACCOMPANIED BY A SUITABLE MILITARY ESCORT – ALL MOUNTED ON ELEPHANTS WHOSE DUTY IT WAS TO CONDUCT THIS SIZEABLE RUBY TO THE PALACE WITH ALL DUE REVERENCE AND SOLEMN CEREMONY.

RIPENING RUBIES

If you were to speak with the gem traders of Bangkok, and if they took a liking to you, they might tell you tales of how the colour of rubies ripens and matures in the ground over many hundreds of years. A good day's trading may encourage them to relate their traditional legend of the fearsome Burmese dragon, Naga, who laid three magical eggs. From the first egg came forth Pyusawti, king of Burma; from the second emerged the great Chinese emperor; and from the third egg flowed all the rubies found to date in Burma – and all those rubies yet to be discovered.

....

THE EDWARDES RUBY CRYSTAL, PROBABLY FROM BURMA; THE LOWER PORTION IS FLAWED

THE *Legends*
◆ OF RUBY

HEALING POWERS

From the 1300s to the 1600s, physicians believed strongly in the power of ruby to preserve the bodily and mental health of its wearer. In the fourteenth century, Sir John Mandeville recorded that whoever owned a ruby was assured of a peaceful coexistence with all men, able to live a tranquil life in the knowledge that his rank and lands would not be taken away from him. Once he had touched the four corners of his lands with his ruby, then his house, vineyard, and orchard would be protected from lightning, tempests and poor harvests. The ruby in question was considered to have greater effect when set in gold and worn on the left side of the body, either as a ring, a bracelet or a brooch.

Camillo Leonardo, physician to Cesare Borgia, wrote of ruby's ability to remove evil thoughts, control amorous desires, dissipate pestilential vapours and reconcile disputes. And a certain Dr Schroeder's *Complete Chemical Dispensatory* (1669) includes the following:

"You may try the goodness of

BELOW: CORUNDUM VARIETY RUBY WITH CUT RUBY CRYSTALS AND GEMS

Rubine by the mouth, and tongue; for the coldest and the hardest are the best. They grow in a stony matrix, of a rose colour, and at first are white, then by degrees growing ripe, turn red.

"As to their virtues: it resists poyson, resists sadness, restrains lust, drives away frightful dreams, clears the mind, keeps the body safe, and, if a mischance be at hand, it signifies this by turning of a darker colour."

UNIVERSAL PANACEA

Throughout the ages, ruby has been thought to banish sadness, dispel nightmares and protect its wearer from plagues – and this is still believed in some parts of the world today. In common with many red stones, it has been universally employed to stem haemorrhage and cure inflammatory diseases. Middle Eastern physicians often prescribed a preparation of finely ground ruby suspended in fruit juice as a means of dispelling fear and promoting joy. The liquid obtained when the stone is bruised in water has also been thought to ease infirmities of the eyes and help disordered livers. As a harbinger of danger, the ruby is said to grow dark when danger threatened, only resuming its previous colour when the danger has passed.

Over the centuries, warriors of several Asian and Malaysian countries became convinced that owning a ruby of fine colour made a man invulnerable to all weapons made of steel, such as the sword, the spear, the dagger and, in recent times, the gun. To achieve this invincibility, fighting men in some areas of Burma will tell you that the stone has to be inserted between the skin and the flesh, in the same manner as the insertion of tabasheer was described by Marco Polo (see pages 118-119).

FAITH, HOPE AND DESTINY

All over the Orient, "star rubies" – those with inclusions that form a star pattern – are looked upon with great veneration. The star is believed to be formed by three benign spirits, imprisoned in the stone for some minor misdemeanour, and their names translate as Faith, Hope and Destiny. These spirits are also believed to dwell in the star sapphire. Those who manage to acquire a good star stone are convinced that their fortunes will change for the better.

A PYRAMID OF SKULLS

The famous Timur Ruby was mined in India. It was owned by the sultans of Delhi and only on special occasions was it taken from the treasury for display. History records that the city of Delhi was invaded, conquered and enslaved by the barbarous Tamerlane of Samerkand. His victory celebrations drew to a terrible climax with the building of a pyramid constructed from the skulls of those he had slain.

This great ruby eventually passed from Tamerlane to the treasury of the great Mogul Jehangir and thence to Shah Jehan, who built the wonderful Taj Mahal palace. It was eventually carried off as loot – along with the Koh-i-Noor, Akbar Shah and other Great Mogul diamonds – by the Persian conqueror Nadir Shah, himself assassinated in 1747.

The Shah of Afghanistan rescued Nadir's heirs from imprisonment, and for that service was rewarded with the fabulous Timur Ruby. After the Sikh wars in the Punjab (1849), it was included in the reparations paid to the East India Company, who eventually presented the stone to Queen Victoria. The Timor is now part of a necklace in the British Royal collection, worn on state occasions by Elizabeth II.

THE *History* ◆ OF THE TIMOR RUBY

CARNELIAN

"Let not the Muse the dull Carnelian slight
Although it shine with but a feeble light."

MARBODUS, BISHOP OF RENNES (11TH CENTURY)

Carnelian is a very attractive and richly hued brownish-red variety of chalcedony. Numbered among the many stones comprising this group are Sard, Heliotrope (Bloodstone, see page 38), Moss Agate (see page 66), Chrysoprase, Banded Agate (see page 66), flint (see page 72) and many others.

Much of the carnelian used today comes from Campo de Maia on the continent of South America, where a sizeable quantity has had the colour improved by staining with ferrous nitrate. Carnelian is also produced in Warwick, Queensland, Australia. However, Ratnapura in India, produces the best quality material.

Carnelian has been known since antiquity. It is said to take its name from the Kornel cherry, which has the same rich colouring. In the 1660s, Dr Johann Schroeder gave another interesting origin. He writes:

"It is a gem half transparent, like the water wherein flesh is washed, or like bloody flesh. Hence it is called 'Carneolus' or 'Carnelian'."

Carnelian is mentioned in Exodus as one of the gems set into the breastplate of the High Priest and as a fundation stone of the New Jerusalem.

ANCIENT WISDOM

The ancients noted how carnelian separated very readily from wax or clay. This phenomenon was given a practical role when carnelian was engraved to make the beautiful intaglio seals used by kings and merchants to authenticate their documents.

The ancient Egyptians are numbered among the many peoples who called upon carnelian as a protective stone. It has been referred to as the "blood of Isis" (the Egyptian goddess of nature) and it was even suggested that it should be cut and shaped in a certain form and then placed at the throat of a corpse at the time of its embalming. The followers of Isis trusted in this powerful talisman to invoke the protection of their goddess any evils that might befall them on their journey through the underworld. Among the talismans and amulets carved from carnelian by the Egyptians were representations of the hand, the fist, the eye, the lion, bee, jackal head, frog and, most often, the bull's head.

THE *History*
◆ OF CARNELIAN

Carnelian was also thought to be the talisman that resisted the onset of bad temper. According to the ancients, bad temper is a form of black magic. As the evil of black magic was often conducted by the light of a waning moon, they believed that the onset of danger could be detected by an unusual sheen over the surface of the protective carnelian.

THE EVIL GLANCE

In most countries of the Middle East, there is a widespread belief that a person looked upon with an ill-meaning or envious glance will lose his fortune.

THE *Legends* ◆ OF CARNELIAN

Wearing a carnelian engraved with an appropriate prayer is said to remove the evil from covetous looks and render them harmless.

HEALING CARNELIAN

Carnelian was once thought to be an excellent remedy for checking bleeding wounds and, according to Dr Johann Schroeder: "The powder of them is good to drink against all fluxes. Carried about, it makes cheerful minds, expels fear, makes courage, destroys and prevents fascinations and defends the body against all poysons. It stops blood by a peculiar property; and bound to the belly keeps up the birth." (1660s) Generally, the healing power of carnelian followed the principle that the appearance of the stone suggested how it could be used – for example, the wearing of almost any yellow stone was prescribed for treating jaundice. Carnelian has also been said to provide the timid with the courage they lack to speak

FACT & FANTASY

VARIOUS ISLAMIC PEOPLES CONSIDER CARNELIAN TO PRESERVE THE EQUANIMITY OF ITS OWNER DURING DISPUTES, AND THEY HAVE ALSO USED SLIVERS OF THE STONE AS TOOTHPICKS. THESE ARE USED BECAUSE THEY NOT ONLY WHITEN THE TEETH, BUT THEY HARDEN THE GUMS AND PREVENT THEM FROM BLEEDING.

boldly and well and to aid astral travel – when placed in front of a light and gazed at intently.

LEFT, A PIECE OF CARNELIAN IN ITS UNPROCESSED FORM. A HARD DARKENED CRUST COVERS THE GLOWING ORANGE CRYSTALS. OPPOSITE ARE THREE EXAMPLES OF THE STONE AFTER PROCESSING AND POLISHING

CAT'S EYES

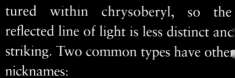

"Those who engage in the practice of litho-healing say that tiger-eye is an effective talisman against hypochondria and all forms of psychosomatic ailments"

URSULA MARKHAM, IN *CRYSTALS & STONES*

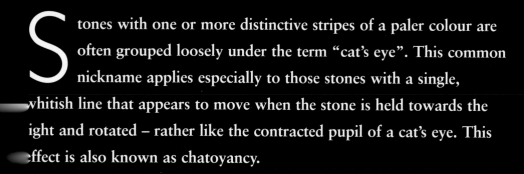

Stones with one or more distinctive stripes of a paler colour are often grouped loosely under the term "cat's eye". This common nickname applies especially to those stones with a single, whitish line that appears to move when the stone is held towards the light and rotated – rather like the contracted pupil of a cat's eye. This effect is also known as chatoyancy.

CLASSIC CAT'S EYES

Various different minerals display this tendency, which is much clearer when stones are cut as cabochons. True cat's eye stones, however, are made of a hard mineral called chrysoberyl, and cat's eye chrysoberyl may also be called cymophane. Chrysoberyl derives its name from the Greek word for "golden", as the usual colouring is a beautiful golden yellow. The stone was known in antiquity and has been remarked upon by Pliny.

The stripe in cat's eye chrysoberyl comes from thin crystalline rods or fibres, laid down in a parallel formation within the stone at the time of its formation, which reflect light in a highly unusual fashion. The finer the quality of these inclusions, and the greater the quantity, the more dramatic the reflective stripe will be. To get an idea of the effect, try looking at the vertical line of light reflected from a reel of silk or cotton.

QUARTZ CAT'S EYES

Several types of quartz are also common cat's eye stones, although their rod-like inclusions are not as fine as those cap-tured within chrysoberyl, so the reflected line of light is less distinct and striking. Two common types have other nicknames:

• "tiger's eye" is an attractively glossy quartz, with golden-brown and yellow stripes, rather like those of a tiger. Originally, cat's eye quartz was a bluish-coloured mineral called crocidolite whose fibres were replaced with quartz. It is the remains of the crocidolite that produce a cat's eye effect and, in the tiger stone, oxidization of the iron in these remains causes a colour change to golden-brown.

FACT & FANTASY

CAT'S EYE ALEXANDRITE IS A RARE AND VALUABLE FORM OF CHRYSOBERYL THAT APPEARS GREEN IN DAYLIGHT AND RASPBERRY RED UNDER ARTIFICIAL LIGHT. ALEXANDRITE WAS FIRST DISCOVERED IN THE URAL MOUNTAINS, ON THE BIRTHDAY OF TSAR ALEXANDER II – HENCE THE NAME.

THE *Legends*
◆ OF CAT'S EYES

"hawks-eye" quartz; here, the bluish colour of the original stone has remained.

VALUED CHARMS

The Assyrians used all kinds of cat's eye stones in effigies of their gods and various peoples through history have believed these stones to be sacred and have valued them as charms against witchcraft and sorcery.

The cat's eye has always been greatly valued in India, where it is regarded as a bringer of wealth – and a talisman to prevent the loss of wealth. The stone is thought to encourage a sense of

---

FACT & FANTASY

THE NINETEENTH-CENTURY KING OF ITALY, VICTOR EMANUEL, SEEMS TO HAVE HAD MANY PECULIAR HABITS. AMONG THESE WAS ALLOWING ONE OF HIS TOENAILS TO GROW TO A LENGTH OF AROUND TWO CENTIMETRES BEFORE FINALLY CUTTING IT AND MAKING IT INTO A TYPE OF "JEWEL". A JEWELLER WAS COMMISSIONED TO CUT AND POLISH THIS NAIL, WHICH THEN ACQUIRED THE APPEARANCE OF A CAT'S EYE STONE, BEFORE FRAMING IT IN GOLD AND PLACING IT IN A DIAMOND SETTING. THE KING PRESENTED THIS STRANGE JEWEL TO HIS MISTRESS, THE COUNTESS MIRAFIORI, WHO EVENTUALLY POSSESSED AROUND 14 SUCH GIFTS!

---

humour and assist in childbirth (see pages 132-135), while applying it to the throats of children suffering from whooping cough will help them to bring up phlegm.

Cat's eyes are believed to protect children from evil spirits, cure rheumy eyes if applied to them as a powder (obtained by burning), and keep teeth clean when rubbed over them thoroughly. Applying the powder is also said to heal sores, causing new flesh to appear in place of the putrid matter.

TOPAZ

"It is judged to be of a Solary Nature by the signature, and is thought to remove night-fears and melancholy, and strengthen understanding, and oppose troublesome dreams (tyed to the left arm, or hung about the neck, and set in gold)."

DR JOHANN SCHROEDER, IN HIS
COMPLEAT CHYMICAL DISPENSATORY, 1669

Topaz is made up of hard, pyramid-capped crystals that belong to the orthorhombic system. The crystals are a combination of fluorine and hydroxyl and the varying amounts of these constituents produce several differently coloured forms, each with its own refractive qualities.

A QUESTION OF COLOUR

Colourless stones are often used as substitutes for diamonds, and they have a similar SG (Specific Gravity) to diamond, although their RI (Refractive Index) and their "fire" (the way they disperse light and sparkle) are much lower. Blue stones have the same SG and RI as colourless ones, and are often mistaken for aquamarine, while yellow, brown and pink varieties have a

lower SG and a higher RI than their colourless and blue relatives. It is the yellow, sherry-coloured stone that is recognized as being the true gem colour.

Red and pink topaz are rarely found, although some specimens have recently been discovered in Pakistan. Generally, delicate pink topaz is the product of 'gem cooks', who heat-treat brown topaz crystals in makeshift ovens. This is known

THE *Legends*
◆ OF TOPAZ

A CRYSTAL OF IMPERIAL TOPAZ – THIS SPECIMEN MEASURES 14 X 4 CM AND WAS FOUND IN VERMELHAO'S MINE, OURO PRETO, BRAZIL
....

as "pinking" and overheating produces a salmon-like colour. This process was discovered in 1750 by a Parisian jeweller who found that applying moderate heat to yellow Brazilian topaz turned it pink. Virtually all pink jewellery topaz used today is the product of heat treatment

Important topaz mines are found in Minas Gerais, Brazil; the Ural mountains of Russia; Sri-Lanka; Zimbabwe; Nigeria; SW Africa; San Diego, USA; and Cornwall, England. The crystals are also recovered from the Mountains of Mourne, in Ireland.

ANCIENT GOLD

Golden topaz, now considered to be the true topaz gemstone, was not recognized by the ancients. In antiquity, all transparently golden stones were called "Chrysolite", possibly from the Greek words *kreusos* (gold) and *lithos* (stone) or the Latin *crisos* (gold) and *oletus* (whole), which give the meaning "wholly gold". Chrysolite also included yellow-green stones and green peridot.

In their manuscripts, the ancients tell us how the finest chrysolites were found exclusively on an island known by the chilling name "Serpent Isle", floating in the Red Sea. Pliny called this same island Topazos – from *topazein*, meaning "to conjecture" – because it was difficult to find. And the Crusaders knew it as the Isle of St John. This volcanic island is shown on modern nautical maps as the Isle of Zebirget, placed around 300 kilometres east of Aswan, in Egypt.

EXCLUSIVE RIGHTS

At some point in the distant past, the mighty Egyptian pharaohs gave the islanders an exclusive licence to collect topaz stones. The islanders guarded this privilege extremely jealously – so much so, in fact, that they posted armed men along the coast with strict orders to sink strange boats and put to death all who attempted an unauthorized approach.

The legend continues that even those

with permission to gather the precious chrysolites could not see the gems in daytime. Only when daylight dissolved to night would the stones be discovered, as their radiance "shone like beacons in the dark." And so, by night, the chrysolite gatherers marked the positions of the stones, and by day, they set out to collect them. They also collected green chrysolites (peridot), believing them to be emeralds.

HEALING PROPERTIES

According to Epiphanius of Cyprus (AD 315-403), the chrysolithos (topaz) occasionally exuded a milky fluid. This fluid, he recommended, should be gathered and used as the antidote for rabies. A number of physicians of the fifth and tenth centuries also claimed to have proved that this treatment was effective.

Roman physicians touched the skin of plague victims with chrysolite (topaz) to treat serious skin ulcers while Marbode, Bishop of Rennes (1067-1081) recommended the wearing of a chrysolite as a pendant. However, only if it were strung on a hair taken from an ass's mane would it guard against evil spirits and nightmares. In the *De Gemmis et Coloribus* of Jerome Cardan (1587), the many virtues of chrysolite included its ability to cure madness and increase wisdom, "thereby resulting in prudence".

COOLING DOWN

Because of the efficient cooling properties of the stone (thrown into boiling hot water, it was said to cool rapidly) topaz was once a cure for frenzy, lunacy, anger, sorrow, fear, melancholy and illusions. It kept enchantments at bay and apparently banished haemorrhoids, averted sudden death, stopped blood gushing from a haemorrhaging wound and dissipated flatulence. Albertus Magnus (1193-1280) describes the stone as being of great assistance in diminishing and eventually curing the pain and damage caused by gout.

In his *Compleat Chymical Dispensatory* of 1669, Dr Johann Schroeder writes:

"The chrysolith, of the ancients, called a topaz by modern jewellers, is a gem of a gold colour. There are two sorts, the Oriental and the European; the first exceeds the last in

MARC ANTHONY, ROMAN STATESMAN DURING THE 1ST CENTURY BC, WHEN TOPAZ WAS USED AS A CURE FOR PLAGUE SYMPTOMS

THE *Legends* OF TOPAZ

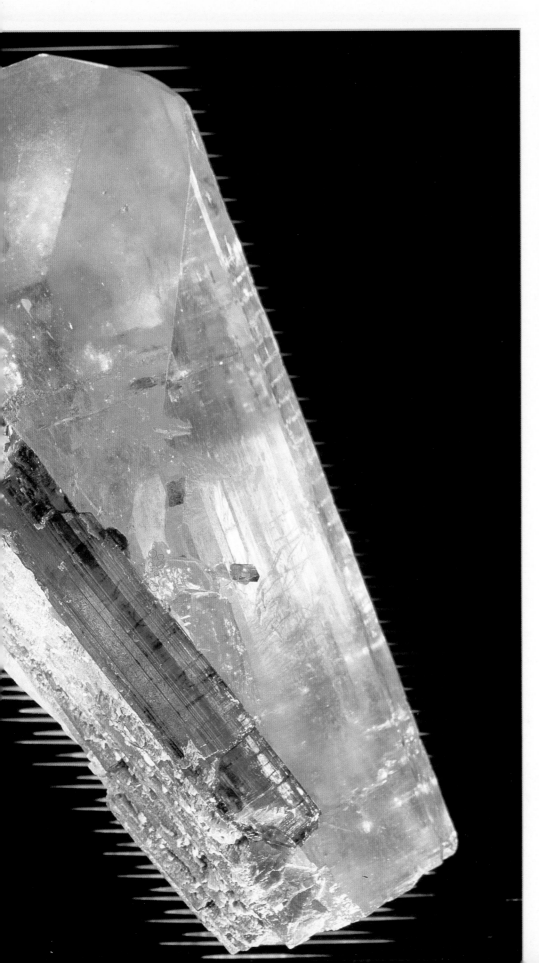

colour and hardness; for this is like crystal, soft; and with the gold colour hath much of the same blackness... Some commend it to be taken against the falling sickness."

VISIONARY POWERS

Widely known and recommended by physicians in the Middle Ages was an eye lotion that claimed to reverse "dimness of the vision"; it was formulated by St Hildergarde, Abbess of Bingen. The eye lotion was prepared by steeping topaz in wine for three days and three nights and was claimed to have an effective life of five days. Before going to bed at night, the patient was required to rub his or her eyes with the lotion so that it touched the eyeball lightly. Topaz was also used by the Ancient Greeks who set it into the tips of long wands to divine the whereabouts of gold and other precious metals.

• •

CRYSTALS OF BLUE TOPAZ AND GREEN TOURMALINE – TOPAZ CAN OCCUR IN MANY COLOURS

BLOODSTONE

"No hope had they of crevice where to hide,
Or Heliotrope [bloodstone] to charm them
out of view."

FROM *THE INFERNO*, BY DANTE (1265–1321)

With its blood-red spots of iron oxide, bloodstone is considered one of the most attractive of the green jaspers. Its old name – heliotrope – is derived from two Greek words , *helios* (the Sun) and *tropos* (to turn). This combination of words refers to an ancient observation that, when immersed in water, the stone captured the sun above as a blood-red image. Pliny went on to say that, out of water "the same stone catches the sunlight like a mirror and detects solar eclipses, showing the passage of the moon as it approaches the sun's disc."

According to a certain legend about the crucifixion of Christ, blood flowing from one of his wounds splashed on to dark green jasper lying at the foot of the cross – and from this sprang the bloodstone variety of jasper. This legend lasted through the Middle Ages and beyond and various sculptors have very skilfully carved the head of Christ in bloodstone so that the red

THE *Legends* ◆ OF BLOODSTONE

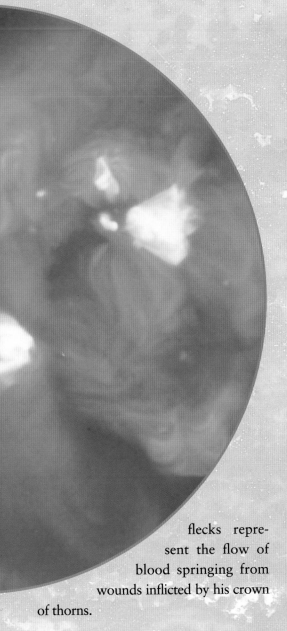

here from the 1600s). According to the writer Menardes:

"The vertue of this stone is much above that of any other gem, for it stops the flux of blood in any part. We have seen some that were troubled with the flux of the Haemorrhoids who found remedy wearing rings made of the bloodstone continually on their fingers."

An old Spanish manuscript on the West Indies notes:

"They do bring from the New Spain a stone of great virtue, called the 'Stone of Blood'. This Bloodstone is a kind of jasper, of divers colour, somewhat dark, full of sprinkles of blood, these being the colour of red. Of these the Indians make certaine Hartes, both great and small; the use thereof, both there and here, is for the fluxes of blood and of wounds."

PURE MAGIC

According to Leonardus, physician to the Borgias, "if it [bloodstone] be rubbed over with the juice of the herb of the same name [see box], it deceives the sight in such a manner as that it renders the bearer of it invisible. The virtue of it is, to procure safety and long life to the possessor of it, and likewise stops the flux of blood. Poisons also submit to it."

Professor Francis Barrett, in his *Celestial Intelligencer* of 1801, continues the widespread fable of the stone's magical properties when he writes:

"The Stone Heliotropium, green, like a Jasper, or Emerald, beset with red flecks, makes the wearer constant,

flecks represent the flow of blood springing from wounds inflicted by his crown of thorns.

THE STONE OF BLOOD

The healing properties of bloodstone, known by physicians as Lapis Sanguinarius, were employed for centuries by the native peoples of South America (known as New Spain by European colonialists, who were moving

FAR LEFT: THIS FROG WAS CARVED FROM BLOODSTONE BY PAUL DREHER. BLOODSTONE IS GREEN AGATE WITH RED JASPER SPECKLES

renowned, and famous, conducing to long life; there is likewise another wonderful property in this stone, which is, that it so dazzles the eyes of men, that it causes the bearer to be invisible: but then there must be applied to it the herb bearing the same name, that is Heliotropium or the Sunflower."

EMERALD

"Who first beholds the light of day

In Spring's sweet flowery month of May

And wears an Emerald all her life,

Shall be a loved and happy wife."

ANON, 1898

Emerald is a variety of beryl, which is a silicate of aluminium and beryllium, and its crystals belong to the hexagonal system. Emeralds owe their green colour to some of the aluminium ions in the crystal lattice being replaced by chromium ones during formation. This gem is rarely found as clean crystals – they are mostly badly flawed.

THE QUEEN OF SHEBA

Emerald had been known to the Ancient Egyptians and other civilizations since before 2000 BC, and most of these emerald mines were in the vicinity of Upper Egypt, near the Red Sea. Most notable of all the mines in this area, situated in Mount Zabarah, supposedly belonged to the Queen of Sheba. Here, the miners believed that evil spirits guarded the emerald treasure, while legend tells of stones from this mine increasing or diminishing in size according to the seasons, and their colour varying with the phases of the Moon.

For many centuries, the mine lay deserted and unworked because its location had been lost. The site was rediscovered after an Egyptian civil service department engaged a French traveller and explorer called M. Caillaud.

Caillaud to find the ancient site. He located the mine in 1818 and made notes and drawings of the tools that he found lying abandoned there. It seemed reasonable to him, he said, to assume that miners of a later period had discovered the mine and continued to work the tunnels long after the Queen's miners had ceased to dig.

SPIRITUAL MATTERS

Revealed in *The Book of the Dead* is a passage that records how the Ancient Egyptians received the gift of emerald from the great god Thoth. Its colour was a reminder of Spring, and so the stone was dedicated to eternal youth. For this reason, *The Book of the Dead* instructed

....

THE QUEEN OF SHEBA OWNED EMERALD MINES IN UPPER EGYPT, SHOWN HERE WITH KING SOLOMON

THE *History* OF EMERALD

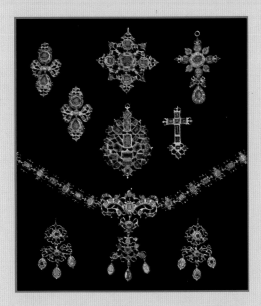

LAVISH EMERALD AND GOLD
JEWELLERY, DATING FROM
EIGHTEENTH-CENTURY SPAIN
....

body embalmers to place emeralds at the throat of every mummy. This ensured that the limbs of the soul maintained a youthful strength during its long journey through the underworld, and was protected from harm.

The gem was also important to the history of various religions, including Christianity, and acquired a mantle of mystic religious significance. For example, like other gems, emeralds were carried or set into amulets and worn in order to keep the wearer focused on spiritual matters. The Christian bishop of Caesarea, Andreas, dedicated the emerald to Saint John the Apostle, and his ability to soothe the souls of sinners.

It is said that 12 different gemstones were set into the breastplate of the great Hebrew High Priest, each engraved with the name of one of the 12 tribes of Israel. One of the gems was an emerald, bearing the name of Gad. Similarly, the New Jerusalem was reputedly built on 12 foundations "garnished with all manner of precious stones" – emerald being the fourth foundation.

As a focus for religious thought, Muslims also use jewels, and emeralds represent their first heaven; in India, presenting an emerald to a god brought with it knowledge of the soul and of eternal life.

THE CONQUEROR'S STONE

During, and long after, the many crusades to the Holy Land, the word emerald was used simply to describe any green gemstone – most people were unaware that there were different types. Vast quantities of green stones thought to be highly valuable gems were traded by the Crusaders or taken as plunder and set into crowns, coronets, and body ornaments. Mostly, these stones were chrysolites, now usually called peridots. Many of the stones proudly displayed as emeralds in European cathedrals and castles would probably be identified by gemmologists as peridots.

THE DAY OF THE CONQUISTADORES

The Spanish Conquerors who overran South America during the sixteenth century were also said to have come upon emerald treasure. The native inhabitants of the

....
A LONG, PRISM CRYSTAL OF EMERALD,
EMBEDDED IN CALCITE

Manta valley in Peru owned a vast emerald that struck awe into all who were privileged enough to see it. The stone was the size, so legend says, of an ostrich egg, and was often referred to as the Goddess Esmeralda and worshipped by the people at their various religious festivals. As many of the Goddess's "daughters" (small emeralds) as the congregation could afford to give were presented to her as offerings.

At the time of the conquest of Peru, the Spanish army sacked the Temple of the Sun and removed from it a large collection of emeralds – but there is no record of them finding the Temple of Esmeralda. To keep their goddess from the grasp of the Conquistadores, the high priests hid the object of their devotion so efficiently that, even to this day, Esmeralda and her temple have not been recovered.

THE *Legends*
◆ OF EMERALD

The home of the legendary Esmeralda treasure was also home to some fascinating beliefs about emeralds. Peruvians believed that emeralds "ripened" just as fruit does, that it began as a colourless stone and gradually became green, with the colour change starting at the corner that faced the Sun.

A CURE FOR ALL ILLS

According to Dr Rowland, working in the seventeenth century, salts and tinctures of emerald "doth wonders in dysenteries and other fluxes, and is good in diseases of the heart and head, in palpitation, melan cholie, phrensie, syncope."

Eastern physicians had an even longer list of things that emerald could alleviate:

- it cured epilepsy
- removed all bodily and mental pains
- stopped vomiting and purged blood
- was an antidote to poison and bites from wasps, bees and scorpions
- allayed unhealthy thirst (diabetes)
- was a remedy for jaundice, liver complaints generally and stricture
- could treat leprosy when finely ground and applied as a poultice.

Because of their colour, emeralds have also been linked with the Roman goddess of the forest, Diana (Artemis in Greek mythology), also considered the guardian of women and young girls and the patron of childbirth. And so, for their connection with Diana, emeralds are credited as talismans that have the power to preserve pregnant women from harm and ensure an easy birth.

EMERALD EYES

In his *Historia Naturalis*, Pliny mentions a marble memorial that stood on the burial mound of a Cypriot prince named Hermias. The

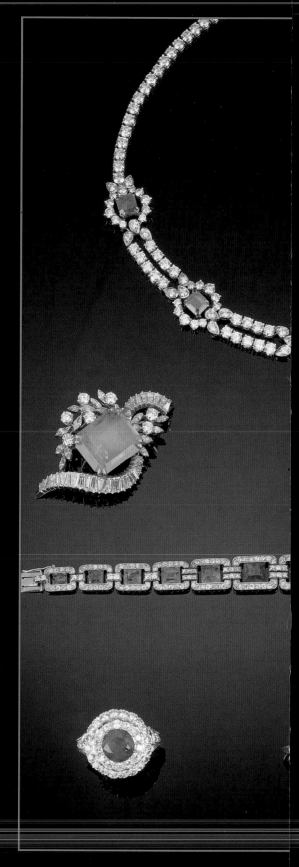

EMERALDS ARE TALISMANS OF
PREGNANCY AND CHILDBIRTH

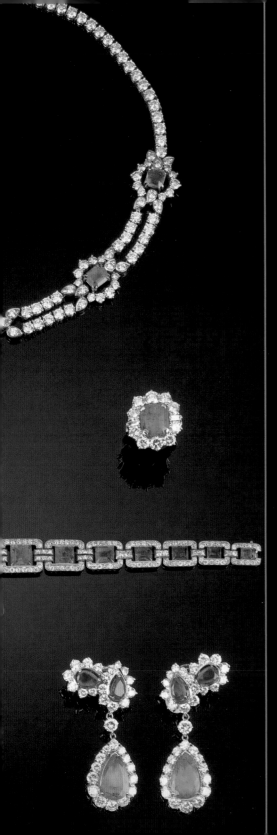

memorial was in the form of a marble lion, and the mound overlooked fishing grounds where tuna fish were caught. This marble lion had emeralds inserted into its eye sockets and these, the legend says, blazed so brightly, "even below the sea", that the tuna fled in terror.

Local fishermen puzzled over their fruitless labours for many months until they realized that the emerald eyes of the statue could be the root cause. They insisted on the removal of the emerald eyes, which were exchanged for different green stones – the fish, Pliny notes, soon returned to the fishing grounds.

That snakes and serpents are blinded when they gaze upon the polished green lustre of an emerald is recorded by the notable seventeenth-century authority on gemstones, Ahmed-ben-Abdalaziz, in his *Treatise on Jewels*. That same legend still lives on today – particularly in the Middle and Far East.

When it comes to human eyes, the doctors of antiquity had an unshakeable belief in the power of emerald to relieve or cure inflammation and infection, and treatment often consisted of placing emeralds on the eyes of patients.

Emeralds have also been thought to enhance sight. Emperor Nero used an eyeglass fashioned from a large emerald crystal to read the many documents that arrived in his office and is also reported to have used the eyeglass to view gladiatorial games held at the Colliseum.

In actual fact, the inclusions found in emerald would make it impossible to find any crystal clear enough and large

FACT & FANTASY

- EMERALDS WERE DEDICATED BY THE ANCIENT ASTROLOGERS TO MERCURY, THE WINGED MESSENGER, AND THE STONE WAS CARRIED BY TRAVELLERS AND SAILORS AS A SPECIAL TALISMAN TO SMOOTH THE ROAD, CALM THE SEAS AND BRING GOOD FORTUNE TO THEIR VENTURES.
- IN ANCIENT TIMES, PARENTS WISHING TO KEEP CHILDREN SAFE FROM THE TWIN SCOURGES OF LEPROSY AND PLAGUE HUNG EMERALD PENDANTS ABOUT THEIR NECKS.
- EMERALD TALISMANS WERE OFTEN USED IN THE EXORCISM OF DEMONS AND DEMONIACAL POSSESSION.
- EMERALD HAS LONG BEEN A LOVER'S EMBLEM – THE STONE WAS CLAIMED TO LOSE ITS COLOUR IF A PARTNER HAD BEEN UNFAITHFUL.
- DREAMING OF AN EMERALD MEANS A BRIGHT FUTURE AND A RENEWING OF OLD FRIENDSHIPS.

enough to form Nero's legendary eyeglass. Instead, it was probably made from pale aquamarine or colourless beryl, which was used for eyeglasses until glass and other materials appeared on the scene.

A SOOTHING SIGHT

Green has often been considered to be a soothing colour. Actors resting in the "green room" of a theatre declare that its green walls repair frayed nerves and soothe eyes strained by powerful stage lights. Tradition also tells of engravers who suffered from eyestrain gazing upon an emerald crystal from time to time to soothe their eyes.

JADE

"In the smoothness of the stone, man recognized Benevolence; in its high polish it captures Knowledge and Education; In the strength and firmness of the material, Righteousness is embraced; in its rarity, Purity is observed; in its stability, Endurance is granted."

KWAN CHUNG, SCHOLAR, SEVENTH CENTURY BC

U ntil the 1800s, jade was thought to be just one stone, but we now know that there are two types – nephrite and jadeite. Similar in appearance, both are fine and hard enough to have been carved into cutting tools and weapons by the ancients and to have been used for all kinds of carvings ever since.

JADEITE

Jadeite was recognized as a separate mineral in 1863, by the French chemist Damour, who analyzed two separate specimens of jade from China and found them to be different minerals. Since nephrite was firmly established, he called the second specimen jadeite.

This, the most precious and rarer of the two jade forms, is also the hardest. It is a tough, compact and finely grained member of the pyroxene group; a crypto-crystalline rock that belongs to the monoclinic crystal system.

Jadeite's colours range through white, pink, yellow, mauve, green and black. The most sought-after colouring is an intense apple green. This eye-catching shade is extremely rare and highly attractive, which is why the Empress of China issued a Royal decree directing that all carvings of apple green jade must be submitted to her Imperial Majesty for inclusion in the royal collection. According to

one report, her collection was housed in 3,000 ivory cabinets. For this reason, apple green jade has come to be known as Imperial Jade. The colour appears as patches in the rock – introduced by the transition element chromium.

....

JADEITE IS THE MOST PRECIOUS OF THE TWO TYPES OF JADE

NEPHRITE

Nephrite is included in the amphibole (horneblende) group and, like jadeite, its crystal system is monoclinic. When viewed under the microscope, this mineral is seen to be composed of fibrous crystals matted and interlocked to form a very tough structure. Its colouring varies from green, grey, or white (the so-called mutton fat), to brown and yellow. Nephrite is often called New Zealand Jade and is far more widespread than jadeite.

JADE SOURCES

China's jade carvings are famous, but for many years the raw material came from elsewhere, and had to be imported into the country. All the early Chinese jade carvings made use of nephrite rather than jadeite. This nephrite came from Turkestan and from the Kuen-Lun mountains, and its recovery from riverbed and rockface, together with the long, difficult journey of nearly 3,000 kilometres to Peking, was an heroic enterprise. In the mid-nineteenth century, boulders of nephrite were discovered in rivers near the southwest end of Siberia's Lake Baikal, and this has provided a much more accessible source of the gemstone.

THE FIRST CHINESE CARVINGS

Only in the 1700s did the Chinese start to carve jadeite, and this came via an equally tortuous journey from Burma, which is still the most important source today.

In 1769, when a written agreement put an end to prolonged wars between China's rulers and the fierce Kachin tribe, some jadeite could be quarried in the jadeite terrain found among the Kachin hills.

Chinese jadeite is now quarried from dykes or collected as water-worn boulders from the Uro River, a tributary of the Irrawady. A most important quarry is at Tawmaw, a village perched nearly 500 metres above the river and just west of Sanka.

The Tawmaw dyke is a large one – it is approximately six metres thick and extends for several kilometres. Quarried jade blocks are taken down to Mogaung and sent from there to Mandalay and Rangoon, and on to Hong Kong, Canton and other Chinese centres.

THE NAMING OF JADE

Yu was the name given to the nephrite transported all the way from eastern Turkestan to reach the master carvers' benches in China. This name also happens to be the general Chinese term for all precious gemstones.

The naming of jade may be traced to the conquest of South America by the famous Spanish Conquistador Cortez. At this time, a hard green stone was being used by the Aztec, Toltec and Olmec peoples as a cure for all manner of kidney diseases, and it was for this reason that the Spaniards called the stone *piedra de ijada*, meaning "hip stone".

From this simple beginning the name jade spread throughout Europe and right across the world.

A MAORI JADE PENDANT FROM THE 1700S. PENDANTS SUCH AS THIS OFTEN BECAME PRIZED CLAN HEIRLOOMS, PASSED DOWN THE GENERATIONS

A legend dating back to the ancient Assyrio-Babylonian era tells the colourful story of the descent of the famous goddess Ishtar to Hades (the underworld).

At each of the seven gates through which Ishtar was obliged to pass, the Guardian of the infernal region directed that an article of clothing or body ornament must be removed. At the fifth gate, the great goddess removed her girdle of jade, a stone said to help when giving birth. It was this legend that led many midwives to adopt the stone as their talisman.

GENERAL TONIC

Around AD 500, Chinese physicians were recommending finely powdered jade to be taken in fruit juice for the relief of heartburn, asthma and the great thirst induced by diabetes.

This drink was prescribed to be taken regularly over a period of time, because it was also said to act as a powerful general tonic that calmed nerves and soothed anxieties. Strengthening the voice and making the hair glossy were just two of its other stated benefits.

The physicians believed that this powder passed through the digestive system unchanged; only the desirable virtues of the stone were absorbed into the body of the patient.

FACT & FANTASY

THE DISTINGUISHED SECOND-CENTURY GREEK PHYSICIAN KLAUDIOUS GALEN WAS PARTIAL TO WEARING A NEPHRITE NECKLACE, WHICH HE SAID HAD THE POWER TO RELIEVE HIM OF STOMACH TROUBLE WHEN IT OCCURRED.

DOCTRINE OF SIGNATURES

Some centuries ago, throughout Europe, pieces of jade tied to the affected part of the body were said to help swollen feet and legs and to bring welcome relief from the pain of kidney stones.

Many physicians of past centuries also subscribed to the "Doctrine of Signatures", by which any material that bore a resemblance to some part of the human body was believed to exert a healing influence on that area. Some of the beliefs about jade ran as follows:

- nephrite of a purplish colour, with bands of yellow and black spots, looked like a section of the spleen and so could exert a healing influence on this particular organ.

- jade with yellow stains and pitting in the midst of a deep purple colour resembled a section of the liver spattered with bile; this was recommended for bilious disorders.

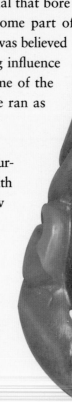

T H E Legends
◆ O F   J A D E

A PENDANT FASHIONED FROM THE MOST HIGHLY PRIZED SHADE OF THIS GEMSTONE – A BEAUTIFUL APPLE GREEN
· ·

• dark red jade, in common with most red stones, was applied to deep wounds to staunch the blood-flow.

As late as the mid-seventeenth century, it was recommended that jade should be tied to the arm or hip or hung about the neck in order to expel kidney stones and treat stomach pains.

WEARING JADE

Jade bangles have been worn by many people in the belief that the stone grants them the physical strength to shrug off impending sickness; jade amulets are especially popular in China, where they are carved into countless different forms, depending on the benefit required. A talisman fashioned in the shape of a padlock is believed to protect children from illness.

There is a popular Chinese legend that tells the story of a butterfly collector. One day, the young man chased a brilliantly coloured butterfly into the garden of a powerful Mandarin, where he met a lovely girl. Instead of being punished for trespassing, the young man won the girl as his bride. Since then, jade butterflies have been exchanged between engaged couples. The eminent Chinese scholar Kwan Chung, who lived during the seventh century BC, concluded that:

• jade's smoothness was a parallel for benevolence
• its high polish suggested knowledge
• its strength and firmness pointed to righteousness
• its rarity equalled purity
• its stability symbolized endurance
• passing it from hand to hand without dirtying the stone stands for upright moral conduct
• the fact that it gives forth a sweet note when struck suggests music.

He concluded that it was these qualities that made people esteem jade and look upon it as a talisman of happiness.

JADE BANGLES HAVE LONG BEEN THOUGHT TO CONFER PROTECTION FROM SICKNESS ON THEIR OWNERS. BEAUTIFULLY CARVED VERSIONS ARE ESPECIALLY POPULAR IN CHINA
· ·

FACT & FANTASY

ONE PARTICULAR ROYAL COURT BOASTED A SET OF STONE CHIMES FASHIONED FROM SMALL SLABS OF JADE. EACH HAD THE SAME LENGTH AND WIDTH; THE MUSICAL NOTE WAS GOVERNED BY THE THICKNESS OF THE SLAB. THESE CHIMES WERE USED AS A PRELUDE TO EVENTS TAKING PLACE AT COURT AND TO HIGHLIGHT RELIGIOUS CEREMONIES.

MALACHITE

BANDED STALAGMITIC MALACHITE FROM ZAMBIA

"[the stone] strengthened the stomach, head and kidneys; it prevented vertigo and rupture and saved the wearer from evil magic, seduction, falls and accidents."

KOZMINSKY, IN *THE MAGIC AND SCIENCE OF JEWELS AND STONES*, 1922

Malachite is a basic copper carbonate, whose green layers resemble the soft green of the marshmallow plant. This has given rise to the stone's name, derived from the Greek word for the plant's colouring – *malache*.

KING SOLOMON'S MINES

Malachite was recovered in large quantities from the mines of ancient Egypt and ancient Israel, which included mines driven into the hills that rose between Suez and Sinai. It was also found in the copper mines of King Solomon, located near Eilat on the Red Sea. Today, an aggregate of malachite, turquoise and chrysocolla is recovered from diggings in this region. This conglomerate rock is cut "en cabochon" into highly popular "Eilat stones", which show blue and green veins when highly polished. Malachite was also highly prized by the Greeks and Romans, who made many jewelled talismans from it.

FROM PAINTS TO PALACES

The use of malachite as an adornment has taken several forms over the centuries. Body jewels and ornaments have been very popular, while the ladies of ancient Egypt used a finely ground malachite powder as a make-up for their eyes, eyebrows, lashes and hair. This same powdered pigment is used by painters under the name "pigment green" or "mountain green".

Architects have long beautified both the exterior and interior of their buildings with polished slabs and mosaics of malachite. Magnificent malachite-faced pillars adorned the grand buildings of tzarist Russia, such as the columns supporting St Isaacs Cathedral, in St Petersburg (formerly Leningrad). The columns supporting St Sophia in Istanbul are faced and decorated in the same fashion.

THE *History* OF MALACHITE

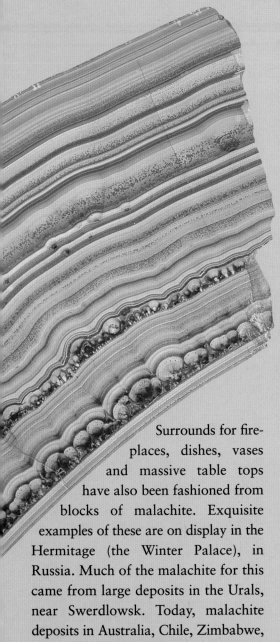

THE *Legends* OF MALACHITE

PEACOCK STONES

On some malachite stones, the complex markings seem to form the pattern of an eye. These specimens are also called "peacock stones", because their colouring and markings resemble the eye-like pattern on a peacock's tail. Because of this, malachite has been worn as amulets, invoking protection from spells cast by the Evil Eye (see page 140). These amulets are especially popular in Italy, where coral hands are also worn to overcome evil influences.

Surrounds for fireplaces, dishes, vases and massive table tops have also been fashioned from blocks of malachite. Exquisite examples of these are on display in the Hermitage (the Winter Palace), in Russia. Much of the malachite for this came from large deposits in the Urals, near Swerdlowsk. Today, malachite deposits in Australia, Chile, Zimbabwe, Zaire, South Africa and the USA provide the bulk of material used for decoration.

MEDICAL MALACHITE

During the seventeenth century, the wearing of a malachite amulet was recommended as a cure for all kinds of ills. The stone was said to avert faintness and prevent hernia, while ground to a fine powder and taken in milk, it reduced the pain of a heart attack and cured colic. If the powder was mixed with honey and smeared over a wound, the flow of blood was said to stop; if taken with wine, it became a cure for virulent ulcers. It seems that malachite amulets and rings have also been worn by mothers and midwives to help promote the teething of infants. Amulets of this type were widely sold in Bavaria

SOME MALACHITE SHARES THE COLOUR AND SHAPE OF A PEACOCK'S MARKINGS

FACT & FANTASY

TO OFFER PROTECTION FROM THE EVIL EYE, MALACHITE SHOULD BE CUT INTO A TRIANGULAR FORM, WHOSE LAYERS SHOW AN EYE-LIKE IMAGE, BEFORE BEING FRAMED IN SILVER. ACCORDING TO THE FRENCH SOCIETÉ DE ANTHROPOLOGIE (1900), A TRIANGULAR TALISMAN SHOWING AN EYE IN THE THREE ANGLES WAS RECOVERED FROM AN ETRUSCAN TOMB AT CHIUSI.

by wandering gypsies.

The stone has also been claimed to boost the health of the stomach, head and kidneys, prevent physical ruptures, banish vertigo and save the wearer from evil magic, seduction, falls and accidents. It is said to bestow strength on children, not only helping them during teething, but also warding off convulsions, guarding them against witchcraft and generally keeping them safe from harm. Malachite has also been called the "sleep stone", for its potential to send wearers to sleep when gazed upon continually.

During the plagues of cholera that often attacked the citizens of ancient Egypt, it was observed that slaves who mined malachite were usually unaffected. From this observation stems the practice of wearing a copper band or bracelet to keep at bay the ravages of rheumatism, asthma and colic.

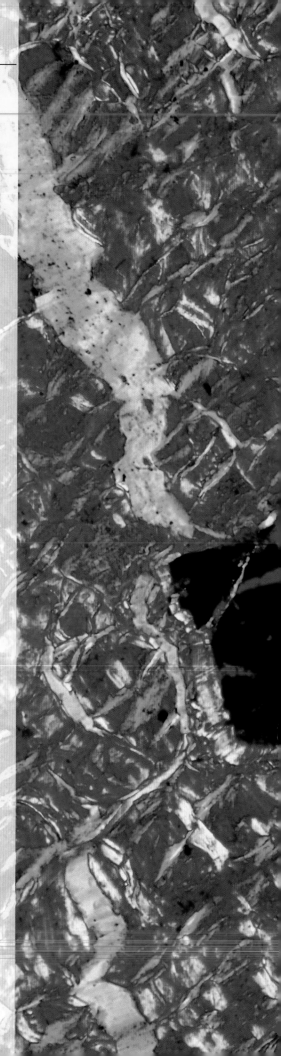

SERPENTINE

"The name serpentine may have been derived from its ancient use as a cure for snake or serpent bite, or it may be because the green and mottled appearance of the stone is similar to that of some snake skins."

CALLY HALL, IN *GEMS AND PRECIOUS STONES*

Serpentine is the general name given to a group of mostly green stones that are made of magnesium silicate. There are two main varieties: bowenite, which is usually a translucent green, and williamsite, which is usually an oily green, with black inclusions. It is softer and rarer than bowenite.

This gem's name seems to be linked to snakes or serpents, perhaps because it looks like snakeskin. The ancients also believed in its talismanic properties as a cure for the poisonous bites of serpents, and so this may also explain the name.

NOT FOR SUNBATHING

Binding small slabs of serpentine to rheumatic joints and limbs was once a fashionable way to relieve the excruciating pains and the stone was also used against dropsy and any complaints caused by an excess of fluids in the body. To enjoy the curative powers of this stone, patients were often told to hold a piece of serpentine in each hand while sitting in sunlight. However, this advice was tempered with a warning to restrict the time spent sunbathing while holding serpentine because of the stone's strong effect on other body fluids.

SCARABS AND SEALS

Serpentine of all colours has been favourably regarded by many civilizations, not only for its power to heal, but also for its beauty as a decorative material. Vases, boxes, talismans and the pillars supporting buildings have all

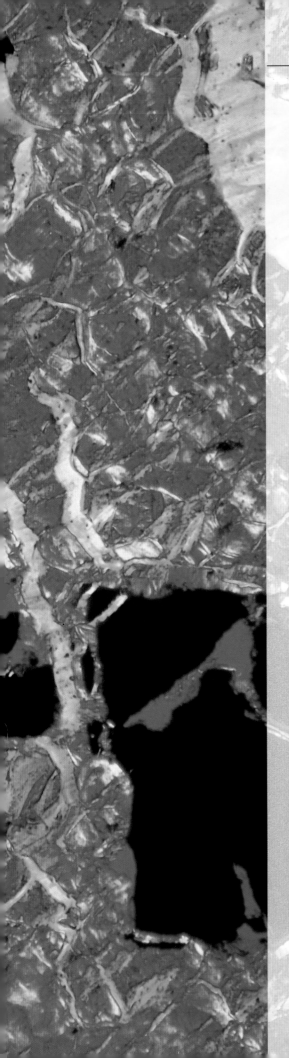

been made from serpentine; the ancient Egyptians carved sacred scarabs from the stone while the Persians produced some beautiful and prestigious serpentine seals.

JADE AND FROGS

There are many different varieties of serpentine, distributed throughout many countries, from the USA to China and beyond.

Samples from the Lizard, in Cornwall, England, usually have a mottling of either green, reddish brown or grey, with patches of other colours; while williamsite from California and Maryland, USA, has blue/greenish colouring.

Green bowenite is often carved into attractive pieces and passed off as jade: under the names "new jade" or "Hunan jade".

Among the fraternity of artists practising their craft in Italy, a particular variety of serpentine is known as *Ranochia*, because this green stone is mottled with paler greens and yellows in a way that resembles the skin of the common frog.

A SCARAB PECTORAL FROM THE TOMB OF TUTANKHAMEN SET WITH STONES

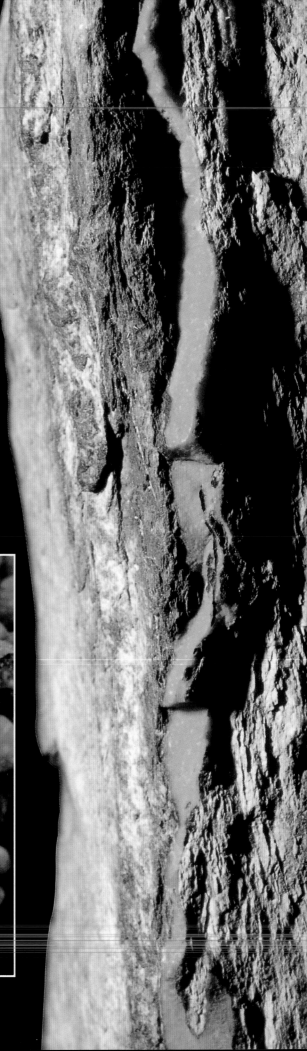

TURQUOISE

"As a compassionate Turquoise that doth tell
By looking pale, the wearer is not well."

JOHN DONNE, POET (1572-1631)

Turquoise is a particularly problematic stone when it comes to verifying its authenticity. It consists of a phosphate of aluminium, coloured by copper and traces of iron. Some gemmologists believe that the beautiful blue colour is produced by a complex ion formed from copper and ammonium. The finest coloured material is mined and worked in Iran; its colours range from the highly desirable sky blue to a bluish green.

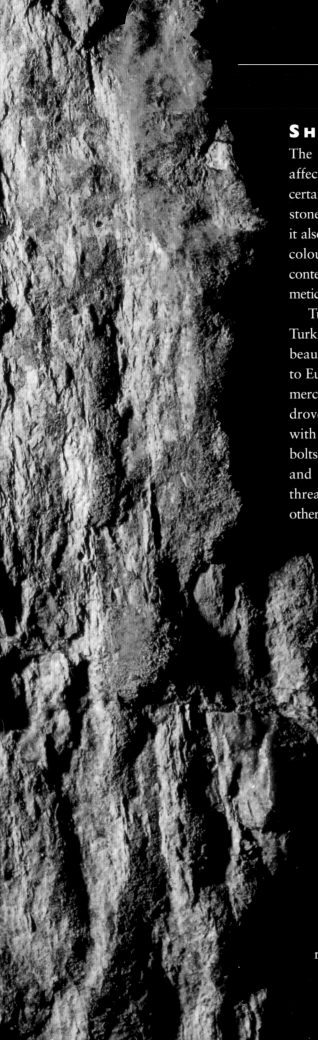

SHADE CHANGE

The colour of turquoise is sometimes affected by the acid perspiration of certain wearers. When this happens, the stone will become green or greenish, as it also does if it becomes too warm. The colour is also affected by the alcohol content in perfume, hair sprays and cosmetics.

Turquoise got its name from the Turkish merchants who first carried this beautiful and very desirable blue stone to Europe for trade. Trudging the commercial trade routes from the East, they drove great camel caravans burdened with sacks of exotic, aromatic spices, bolts of cloth encrusted with gemstones and interwoven with gold and silver threads, and all kinds of jewels and other treasures.

The stones were first exported to Germany, where they became known as *Turkisher Steins*, which translates as "Turkish stones". When the stones reached France, the German name became translated into *Pierre turquoise* – stone of Turkey.

THE PEOPLES OF THE AMERICAS

Many thousands of years BC, forebears of the Aztecs, Toltecs and Olmecs migrated from that vast tract of grassland we now call Mongolia. They crossed the ice bridge formed on the Bering Straits which, at times, joins Russia to Alaska. The tribes roamed farther and farther south until they finally settled in southern America – in and around the lands now called Mexico, Brazil and Peru.

These tribes took with them their reverence for turquoise and their skills to work this beautiful, sky-blue rock. Their talents and ingenuity are evident in the craftsmanship and beauty of the artefacts that have been recovered from ancient tombs, including the death masks skilfully inlaid with turquoise mosaic.

According to the missionary Bernardino de Sahagun (*History of New Spain*, 1830), no one was allowed to wear or own this blue stone: it was exclusively reserved as an offering to the gods and for the decoration of their images. After the decimation of the Mayan Empire by the Spaniard Hernando Cortez in AD 1533, it fell to the lot of the Pueblo people of the American southwest to keep this reverence for turquoise alive. Even today, Pueblo miners believe that the "flesh" of turquoise must remain undamaged; if it is to be used as a religious offering, it must be mined and handled with respect.

Turquoise was also held in very high esteem by the Apache peoples of North America. Indeed, without possession of a turquoise, no medicine-man could command the honour, respect and veneration his office demanded. Nor would the spear or arrow of the hunter fly true to its target.

LEFT: TURQUOISE VEIN IN SHALE FROM VICTORIA, AUSTRALIA. FAR LEFT: WEST PHEONIX MINE, CORNWALL, ENGLAND

man's talisman and it was at this time that a certain man called Volmar wrote: "whomsoever owns a true turquoise set in gold will not injure any of his limbs when he falls, whether he be riding or walking, so long as he has the stone with him."

A HEAVY FALL

The seventeenth-century medical man Anselmus Boetius de Boot gives an account of how, the morning after his horse stumbled and threw him heavily to the ground, he noticed that a large

---

FACT & FANTASY

TURQUOISE IS A SYMBOL OF GENEROSITY, SINCERITY AND AFFECTION.

• IT IS THOUGHT TO PRESERVE FRIENDSHIP AND MAKE FRIENDS OF ENEMIES.

• TO BRING GOOD LUCK, IT SHOULD BE GIVEN, NOT BOUGHT.

• TO DREAM OF TURQUOISE IS TO GREET PROSPERITY.

• IT BRINGS GOOD LUCK ON A SATURDAY.

PROTECTION FROM HARM

Turquoise was once credited with the ability to overcome malevolent glances from the Evil Eye. Even today, the citizens of many Middle Eastern countries weave turquoise beads into the manes and tails of beasts of burden such as camels, mules and oxen to bring good luck and assurance that the animals will be surefooted.

Turquoise beads are also believed to protect a horse if it becomes overheated by too much exertion – and to shield the rider from harm. From the thirteenth century, this stone became the horse-

piece of the turquoise stone in his ring had broken away. He believed that the influence projected by his turquoise had saved him from severe injury.

According to another writer, Van Helmont, "whoever wears a turquoise so that it touches the skin may fall from any height; the stone attracts to itself the whole force of the blow so that it cracks,

THE Legends OF TURQUOISE

and the person is safe." A certain Marquis of Villena had a slightly different story to tell, however. The Marquis employed a court jester who was asked "What are the magical properties of the turquoise." "Why Sire," replied the jester, "Should you climb to the highest rampart of your castle while wearing that stone, and hurl yourself therefrom to the courtyard below – the magic of the stone is that it would remain unbroken."

It was also Anselmus de Boot who wrote of turquoise chiming the hours against the side of a glass when suspended from a thread. On a fashion note, he observed that the best-dressed men considered themselves totally unprepared to step out unless they were wearing a tourquoise jewel.

HEALING PROPERTIES

Many physicians of the fifteenth century carried a turquoise in their medical bags, claiming that the stone would counter the harmful effects of poison. They pre-pared a potion containing finely pow-dered turquoise, which, as well as proving to be a powerful antidote to scorpion stings, was also considered

effective in banishing the pains arising from possession by demons. Looking at a turquoise – or placing a stone on the eyes – was believed to soothe inflamed or strained eyes.

Turquoise indicated the health of the wearer by turning pale if he or she became sick. It lost its colour completely when its wearer died, regain-ing its beauty when it was possessed by a new, healthy owner. Sir John Horsey, a mes-senger in the employ of Elizabeth I, records that Tsar Ivan the Terrible believed that turquoise had a unique empathy with its wearers and showed its sympathy for their sufferings by turning pale. Many eighteenth-century writers contributed to these beliefs when they included in their books such words as "the stone grew pale when there is any peril prepared for him that weareth it."

BLUE SKIES AHEAD

To the Persians, the intensity of the sky-blue stone foretold the kind of weather to be expected that day. A dazzling blue colour seen during the morning foretold a fine day, and a happy one. The Persians also say that to have good fortune and repel evil, a man must see the reflection of the new moon on either a copy of the Koran, the face of a friend, or on a turquoise stone.

LAPIS LAZULI

"He who carries with him into battle an amulet of Lapis carries with him the presence of his god."

A SAYING OF THE
ANCIENT SUMARIAN PRIESTS

The name of this beautiful, decorative material is derived from a medieval Latin form of the Arabic word *lazward*, meaning blue. The later Latin form *lazurius* and the French *azure* are taken, respectively, from the Persian word *lazur* and the Arabic *azul*, each word meaning a very special colour of deep blue.

An analysis of this stone shows it to be a rocklike mixture of several minerals, namely hauynite, lazurite, sodalite, calcite and pyrites. The attractive speckles found in lapis are actually tiny crystals of iron pyrites. It is a metamorphic rock and has often been confused with Azurite – a blue hydrated copper carbonate stone. Another similar rock is the fine-grained, greyish-brown jasper named "nunkirchner jasper", which is found in deposits near Idar-Oberstein. This jasper is stained a lazurite blue colour, which explains its popular nickname – "Swiss Lapis".

PRECIOUS COLOURING

Lapis lazuli does not have a crystalline structure and so by definition cannot be included in the list of precious gems – its value lies in its attractive colouring, which has prompted people to use it as a decorative material from the earliest times. It also has a long history as the material used to make the painter's pigment "Ultramarine".

The best lapis lazuli is still quarried in the province of Badakshan, Afghanistan, just as it was when Marco Polo visited the quarry in AD 1271. The stone is also quarried near Russia's Lake Baikal, while poorer quality lapis comes from Chile and the USA.

THE SAPPHIRE OF ANCIENT GREECE

Ancient manuscripts reveal that the stone was considered the sapphire of ancient Greece – Theophrastus claimed that this "sapphire" was "sprinkled with gold dust" – and all references to sapphires in the writings of antiquity are now taken to mean lapis lazuli.

Medieval troubadours told tales of a priest-king called Prester John (see also page 144), who retired to his sleep on a bed made from a single block of "sapphire" in order "to make him sleep well and destroy lustful thoughts." It was thought that the spirits of light and wisdom were attracted to blue stones because they resembled the blue of the heavens, and that lapis was an emblem of chastity.

STRIKING LAPIS BEADS FORM THE CENTREPIECE OF THIS ARRAY OF JEWELS

POTENT TALISMANS

For those requesting solutions to their problems from the Oracle at the shrine of the god Apollo, it was mandatory for the supplicant to wear a blue sapphire. Necromancers, too, placed great value on the stone – it enabled them to hear and interpret the most difficult predictions of the Oracles. And witches utilized this sky-blue stone to fix enchantments and spells.

A great Greek classic tells the story of Prometheus wearing a sapphire ring when he braved the wrath of Zeus. In this epic he is seen stealing fire from heaven in order to return it for the use of man – mankind having been deprived of fire as a punishment for eating the flesh of sacrificial offerings made to Zeus, the great god of Olympus.

The strong beliefs and practices of various sorcerers held great influence during the Middle Ages, and these magicians terrified the citizens of many towns and villages when they insisted that blue sapphire changed colour to a violet hue in the presence of infidelity. The stone was also reputed to find out fraud, treachery and enchantments, and was claimed to be peerless in providing protection from envy and the revenge of enemies.

THE TALISMAN OF CHARLEMAGNE

According to William Pavitt (*The Book of Talismans*, 1914), a most potent talisman for love was one especially made for the wife of the Emperor Charle-

THE MIGHTY CHARLEMAGNE, "EMPEROR OF THE WEST" (800-814)

magne by the sorcerers of the court of Haroun el Raschid, Emperor of the East. This talisman contained two large cabochon sapphires – one oval and the other square – set into a cross fashioned from a remnant of wood from the Holy Cross. The cross was made for the sole purpose of keeping Charlemagne's affections constant to his wife, and it was so effective that his love for her never diminished.

FACT & FANTASY

THE MOST POTENT OF MAGICAL SAPPHIRES ARE THOSE THAT SHOW ASTERISM. THIS MEANS THAT, UNDER CERTAIN CIRCUMSTANCES, A SIX-RAYED STAR IS VISIBLE IN THE STONE. GEMMOLOGICALLY SPEAKING, THIS STAR IS SEEN WHEN RUTILE NEEDLES – FORMED NATURALLY IN THE SAPPHIRE – ARRANGE THEMSELVES PARALLEL TO THE THREE CRYSTAL AXES AND THE STONE IS CUT AS A CABOCHON.

BUT THIS SCIENTIFIC EXPLANATION MEANS NOTHING TO THOSE WHO LIVE IN THE ORIENT. HERE, STAR SAPPHIRES ARE REGARDED AS LEGENDARY BEARERS OF GOOD FORTUNE. THOSE THREE CROSSING RAYS ARE FERVENTLY BELIEVED TO BE THREE GOOD SPIRITS, FAITH, HOPE AND DESTINY – IMPRISONED WITHIN THE STONE FOR SOME MINOR MISDEMEANOUR. THIS IS ALSO BELIEVED BY THOSE IN THE EAST TO BE THE CASE FOR STARRED RUBIES (SEE PAGE 28).

THE LEGEND TELLS THAT, BECAUSE THE SPIRITS IN THIS BEAUTIFUL STONE ARE CARRIED ABOUT BY ITS OWNERS AND SO CAN ONLY OBSERVE, RATHER THAN TAKE PART IN, WORLDLY AFFAIRS, THEY REWARD THEIR OWNERS WITH SUCCESS IN THEIR DAILY DEALINGS.

AMETHYST

*"The bloodie shafts of Cupid's war
with Ametists they headed are."*

FROM *ARCADIA*, BY SIR PHILIP SIDNEY, POET
(1554-1586)

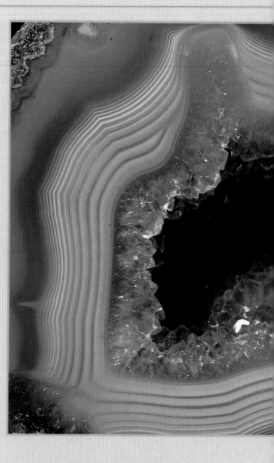

**PURPLE AMETHYST CRYSTALS AND
BANDS OF AGATE LINE THE CAVITY IN
THIS PIECE OF ROCK**
....

The name amethyst is applied to any purplish form of crystal quartz, which consists of silicon dioxide and has a trigonal crystal structure. Like many stones, its history is bound up with religious practices. One of the earliest references to religious usage of the amethyst is of this stone being named as one of the twelve stones set into the breastplate of the High Priest who officiated at the Holy Temple of Jerusalem. According to the Bible, amethyst was also set into the wall of the New Jerusalem.

THE *History* ◆ OF AMETHYST

Those Christian bishops who became elected as Roman senators adopted the colour purple – long associated with high rank – for their robes. And so, over the passage of years, amethyst became the "emblem of celestial regions", representative of these churchmen.

Amethyst was well known to the ancient Egyptians who, in accordance with instructions laid down in the *Book of the Dead*, placed the stone on the body of the deceased. Many specimens of heart-shaped amethyst have been recovered from the tombs of the pharaohs, who not only regarded the heart, quite rightly, as the seat of life, but may have attempted to employ certain para-normal "vibrations" of amethyst in some particular way as yet unknown to the modern world.

"There are," says the philosopher and writer Francis Bacon (1561-1626), in his *Sylva Sylvarum*:

"many things that operate upon the spirits of man by secret sympathy and antipathy. That precious stones have virtues in the wearing has been anciently and generally received, and they are said to produce several effects."

It is not, therefore, surprising to discover that there is a long history of people believing that a stone can affect people's disposition. Especially when

THE *Legends*

◆ OF AMETHYST

vinced that this was the only way to indulge in alcohol; amethyst was believed to exert such an influence on the wine that its alcoholic content was completely neutralized. Others, attempting to explain this apparent effect, took the uncharitable view that their hosts had diluted the wine with water. The violet colour of the amethyst goblet, they said, enhanced the colour of diluted wine and in this way its contents looked genuine.

PROTECTION AGAINST SPELLS

Pliny takes the magi to task for suggesting that people should engrave amethyst with the names of the Sun and Moon, and wear the engraved stones around the neck, together with baboon's hairs and swallow's feathers, as protection against spells. The stone, the magi said, would also assist people to approach a king as a supplicant, as well as keeping away hail and plagues of locusts.

Pliny scornfully writes: "I can only suppose that in committing these statements to writing they express a derisive contempt for

mankind." But the ideas of the magi continued to hold sway.

In 1750, Camillus Leonardus wrote of amethysts:

"their virtue is to drive away drunkenness, for, being bound on the navel they restrain the vapour of the wine and so dissolve the inebriety; they repress evil thoughts and give good understanding; they make a man vigilant in business; the barren they render fruitful by drinking a lotion of it; they expel poison; they preserve military men and give them victory over their enemies; and prepare an easy capture of wild beasts and birds."

light from the stone's tutelary planet is focused by, and through, the gemstone. The radiation of violet light issuing from amethyst has been placed on record as providing a calming influence upon the nerves, and is said to be instrumental in slowing rapid and agitated movements of the wearer's body.

SOBER INFLUENCE

The name of this mineral is derived from the Greek *amethystos*, meaning "non-intoxicating". Over the centuries, ancient Greek and Roman magi, or wise men, claimed that this stone had the desirable power of preventing drunkenness, and it is from this powerful property that its name was derived.

Those of the ancients who drank wine from amethyst goblets were con-

ANTIQUE AMETHYST BRACELET, FROM A MATCHING SET OF JEWELLERY

BACCHUS AND DIANA

An eighteenth-century French poem tells the story of Bacchus, the Greek god of wine. As the story goes, it seems that Bacchus felt that his exalted position in the Universe had been neglected by mortals and swore to have his lions avenge this disrespect by devouring the next mortal to cross his path.

A certain maiden named Amethyst, on her way to worship at the shrine of Diana, became the next unfortunate mortal to come Bacchus' way. Accordingly, the lions set about their grisly task. The piteous screams and desperate struggles of poor, terrified Amethyst reached the ears of the kindly Goddess Diana, who took pity on the distraught maiden. Diana quickly eased the girl's suffering by turning her into a pillar of beautiful, transparent rock crystal.

Bacchus, the poem continues, now regretting his loss of self-control, was overcome with deep remorse. In an effort to make amends, he contritely poured a generous libation of wine over the rock crystal pillar. The pillar then assumed the desirable purple-violet colour of the stone we know as amethyst.

THE *Legends* ◆ OF AMETHYST

CHANDELIER EARRINGS IN A DAZZLING COMBINATION OF DIAMOND AND AMETHYST

SICKNESS OF THE SOUL

The magi of the Middle Ages believed that all sickness of the body arose from a sickness of the soul. To counteract this, they prescribed elixirs containing amethyst in some form, taken together with much praying to particular saints.

In later years, physicians extended the curative powers of the stone to include supposedly effective treatment of headache, toothache and gout; and, in common with many gemstones, it was considered instrumental in protecting the wearer from poison and the plague. Amethyst is also recommended for neuralgia and insomnia.

TALES OF TRUE LOVE

There is one tale of an amethyst being cut and polished into the shape of a heart, set in silver or gold, and given by the bride to her husband.

This heart-shaped amethyst supposedly conferred on the newly married couple the greatest blessings of happiness and tranquillity for the rest of their lives.

LASTING BEAUTY

In Barbara Walker's *The Book of Sacred Stones*, she recounts many legends about amethyst. She concludes that its sheer beauty leads many people to wear just this stone and no other. As an example of this passion, she cites the islanders on Sark, in the English Channel, who sell all amethysts found on the island as "Sark stones".

FACT & FANTASY

◆ THE STONE, DEDICATED TO NEPTUNE, IS WORN BY SAILORS BECAUSE IT GUIDES THEM TO A SAFE HARBOUR.

◆ TO DREAM OF AMETHYST SIGNIFIES THAT YOUR NEXT UNDERTAKING WILL BE SUCCESSFUL.

◆ AMETHYST (OR A STAR SAPPHIRE) IS CARRIED BY SOLDIERS TO PRESERVE THEM FROM HARM AND ENSURE VICTORY.

AGATE

"By the rushing fringed bank

Where grows the willow and the osier dank

My sliding chariot stops

Thick set with Agate."

JOHN MILTON, POET (1608-74)

All lapidaries will, at one time or another, have worked with the type of quartz known as agate – known for its wonderful colours and patterns. He or she will have sawn it, sliced it, ground it, tumbled its pebbles, stained the stone with many attractive colours, and polished it to make the most of its natural features – often turning what seems a dull lump of stone into an object of beauty and admiration.

The many varieties of agate belong to a kind of quartz known as chalcedony. This is a crypto-crystalline quartz, which means that it is composed of a mass of minute crystalline fibres. It has no external crystalline form, but when each kind of chalcedony is viewed under the microscope, its fibrous crystalline structure is clearly visible.

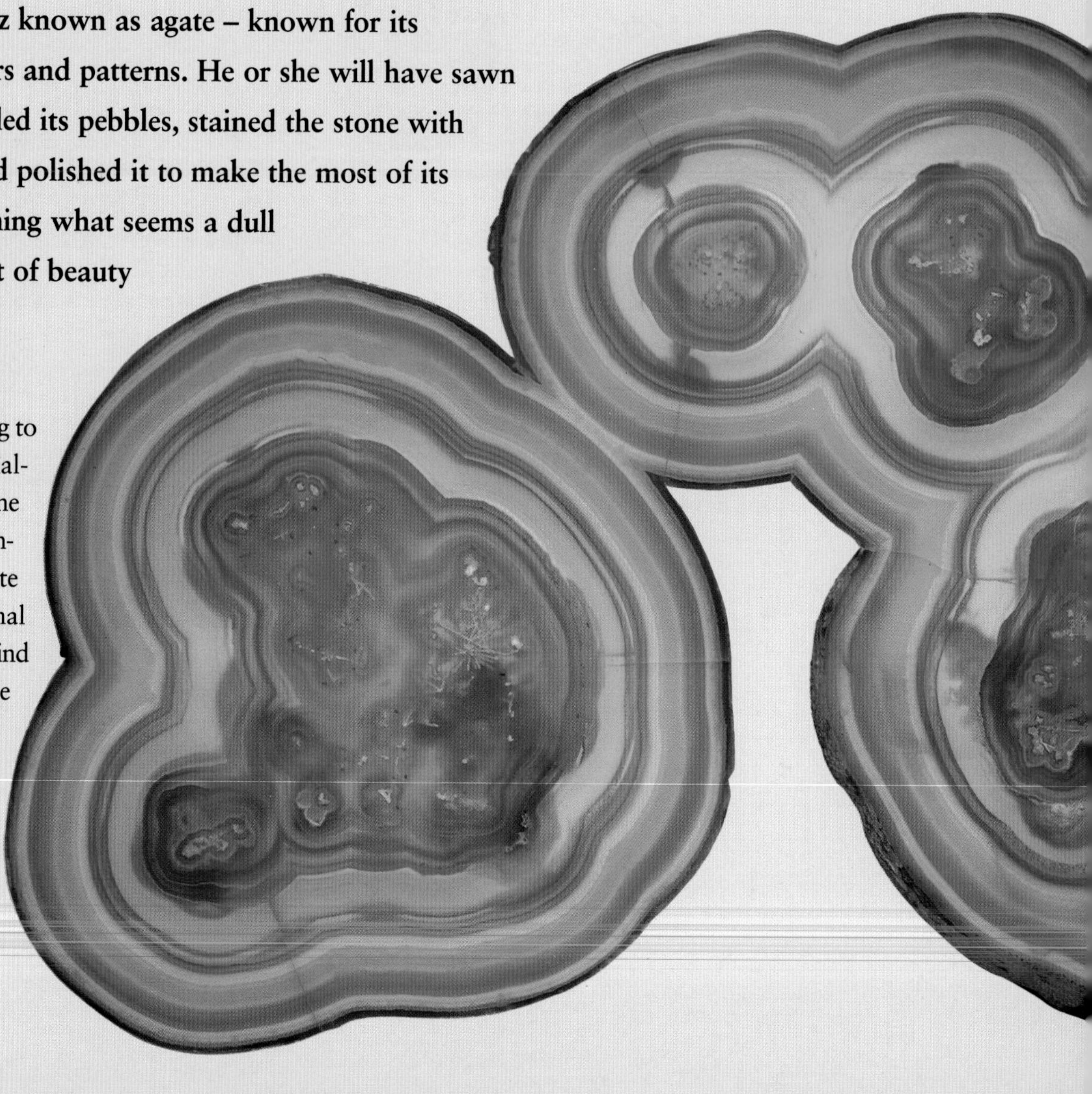

THIS SECTION OF AGATE SHOWS THE TYPICAL PATTERN OF COLOURED BANDS AROUND SEVERAL CENTRES

BANDED PATTERNS

Agate is distinguished from other kinds of chalcedony by its banded patterns – milky, opaline layers that seem to follow the outline of the cavity in which the agate was formed.

Certain kinds of cavities formed in ancient lavas provide the birthplaces of agate. As the laval rocks decompose, rains dissolve and carry various minerals to these cavities where, as the rain water evaporates, they are deposited to form as agate – in any size from pebbles to boulders.

Half Price Books #054
7805 Leary Way
Redmond WA 98052
425-702-2499
Transaction No: 8875
Customer ID:
04/14/98 22:01:30   CLERK: BRIAN

1 @ 9.98 RN   9.98
    New books - bargain prices
SUBTOTAL   9.98
TAX @ 8.600%   0.86
TOTAL   10.84
CASH   11.00
Total Tendered $ 11.00
CASH Credit (amount)   0.16

THANK YOU!
We pay cash for books, music, & software
25 Years of Reading Together

A COLLECTION OF POLISHED "FIRE AGATES". THE IRIDESCENT COLOURS OF THESE STRIKING STONES ARE CAUSED BY IRON OXIDE DEPOSITS

Vast amounts of agate are imported from South American countries such as Brazil and Paraguay, where it is recovered from the red clay of decomposed basalt. The Indian Deccan Valley also has much good-quality agate for export; here the various agates are recovered and collected from weathered basaltic rock.

COLOUR STAINING

Because agate is very porous, it lends itself readily to dyeing and staining. To this end a vast industry has developed, in which huge quantities of very ordinary agate are made especially attractive with the aid of chemicals.

Agates that have been soaked in potassium ferrocyanide and treated with a copper sulphate solution receive a good blue colouring, while soaking agates in a ferrous sulphate produces an attractive red colour after heating. Nickel provides green tints and aniline dyes produce a range of attractive hues. Producing the black colour of onyx is a mere matter of boiling agate in a sugar solution, which enters the pores of the agate and prepares the way for the colour change. There are, however, special cleaning processes that can remove most of the colouring and almost return the stone to its original, natural colour.

PLACE OF ORIGIN

Many of the earliest references to agate are there for students to study in the writings and records of Theophrastus (c.370-285 BC).

In these records, we learn that agate was first named after the River Achates, in which the stones were apparently first discovered and where their potential for decoration was recognized. The River Achates is now known as the River Dirillo, which rises near Mt Lauro and winds its course down through the mountains, eventually draining its waters into the sea at the southern tip of the Mediterranean island of Sicily.

Over many centuries, the seemingly diverse powers of agate slowly revealed themselves to the many ethnic peoples dwelling in the countries bordering the southern coast of the Mediterranean Sea. Here, the stones became talismans that prevented falls and accidents, and those who followed Islam engraved the symbols of the grandsons of the Prophet – Hassan and Hussein – on agate and hung them about the necks of children.

THE History OF AGATE

The Legends ◆ OF AGATE

Just as followers of Islam believed in the power of agate, ancient Jewish folklore also invested it with powerful gifts of protection that prevented its owner from stumbling or falling. This valuable property meant that the stone was highly prized by horsemen, who wove agate into their horses' manes and set it into their harnesses. Later, horsemen in many parts of the world would adopt it as their talisman.

THE SIGN OF THE EYE

Brown and black agates that had been cut and polished in such a way as to show a white oval outline came to be regarded, by many peoples of northern Africa, as a symbol of the eye. They became yet another talisman that was said to protect people from the Evil Eye. Agate eye stones were also in great demand by the citizens of the Syrian city of Alleppo, who were convinced that the stones were a means of alleviating the painful ravages of Alleppo boils – boils that looked uncannily like an eye agate. Eye agates placed upon tired eyes were considered peerless in refreshing them and restoring keen sight.

Eventually, the superstitions surrounding agate were taken up in Europe, where, for example, farmers tied agates to the horns of oxen and the harnesses of horses while ploughing their fields, in the hope that it would bring a bountiful harvest.

MEDICINAL AGATE

Dioscorides, in the fifth and last book of the series entitled *Materia Medica*, describes over two hundred stones used medicinally by physicians in civilian practice and by those accompanying the Imperial Roman armies. It contains descriptions of the virtues of agate, and these continued to exert an influence over the following 1600 years.

For example, in cases of insanity, the recommended treatment was a preparation of powdered agate and sweet fruit juice. The same medicine was also prescribed for ulcers, boils and diseases of the kidneys and spleen.

Certain varieties of agate were employed to stem haemorrhages and to combat the ravages of epidemics and pestilential disease. Worn as pendants, they also gave their wearers protection from indigestion, lung problems and fears of all kinds.

Some Arabian physicians advised against the practice of using powdered agate for internal medicines, although they were certain that a paste of powdered agate arrested the bleeding of tender gums and made them much tougher.

WITCHES, WARLOCKS AND LIGHTNING

In Camillo Leonardo's *Speculum Lapidum* of 1502, readers will find a reference to the ability of agate to avert the destructive powers of tempest and lightning.

In England, in the Midlands and in northern areas, these beliefs live on. Here, farmers will drive a nail into the woodwork over the door of the dairy and suspend from it an agate that has a hole naturally bored through it. This superstitious ritual is thought to prevent thunder and lightning turning the milk sour and to put a stop to witches and warlocks riding cows and horses roughshod over the countryside in the dead of night.

FACT & FANTASY

A BANDED AGATE WITH LIGHT AND DARK AREAS EITHER SIDE OF A CENTRAL CAT'S EYE STRIPE IS KNOWN BY SOME AS THE STONE OF SYLVESTER OR THE STONE OF ST JAMES. THE LIGHT SIDE OF THE STONE REPRESENTS THE PAST, AND THEREFORE ALL KNOWN EVENTS, WHILE THE DARK SIDE REPRESENTS THE DARK VEIL OF THE UNKNOWN FUTURE, WHICH SHROUDS EACH PERSON'S KNOWLEDGE OF THEIR DESTINY. AT ONE TIME, IT WAS THE CUSTOM FOR THESE STONES TO BE GIVEN AND RECEIVED AS NEW YEAR'S PRESENTS; THEY WERE ALSO PRESENTED TO THOSE BORN ON ST JAMES OR ST SYLVESTER'S DAY.

References to some of agate's magical powers are found in the histories and legends of the Vikings and the peoples of Saxon England. In these communities, a magical double-headed axe and a round agate were used to find lost articles or buried treasure. The name for this kind of magical divination is axinomancia,

AGATE IS SAID TO STILL THE POTENT FORCES OF THUNDER AND LIGHTNING

and the ceremony is performed as follows. A double-headed axe was heated until it glowed red. It was then placed in an upright position by pushing the handle into a hole in the ground, and the round agate pebble was placed carefully on the glowing axe head. If the agate pebble stuck to the axe head, then the seeker of lost treasure must look elsewhere; if the stone fell to the ground, then they must follow the direction in which the stone rolled to find their quarry.

BRINGER OF SLEEP

Wearing agate rings and pendants has been recommended to bring sound sleep and calm, content waking hours, as well as an agreeable manner, good health and long life. Dreaming of agate suggests a journey by sea and the stone has also been said to prevent seasickness.

TOURMALINE

"To the same class of fiery red stones belong the 'lychnis' [probably tourmaline] so called from the kindling of lamps, because at that time it is exceptionally beautiful... I find that there are other varieties as well, one of which has a purple and the other a scarlet sheen. These when heated in the sun or being rubbed between the fingers, are said to attract straws and papyrus fibres."

PLINY THE ELDER (AD 23-79)

Tourmaline is a complex boro-silicate of aluminium and various other metals – its scientific formula consists of fifty characters. It contains long, prismatic crystals that have a rounded triangular shape in cross section, with strong striations along its length.

RAINBOW SHADES

Because of its variety of colours, tourmaline is easily confused with many precious gems. This relatively inexpensive stone has the greatest colour range of all the gemstones – colourless, pink, green, blue, brown, and all kinds of intermediate shades. There is also an attractive and unusual purplish colour known as "Siberite" – a name reserved for crystals found in the Russian Ural Mountains.

Parti-coloured stones of two or three colours are quite common – for example, pink at one end, colourless in the centre, and green at the other end of a crystal or faceted stone. Some crystals, when cut across their width, will show a pink centre surrounded by a green border, looking very much like a slice of watermelon. This "Watermelon Tourmaline" comes mainly from Brazil.

Brazil is also home to an attractive, intense emerald green stone – popularly known as "Brazilian Emerald". Known, too, by the name chrome green tourmaline, this could be confused with genuine emerald by the general public. At one time, this variety of green tourmaline was consecrated and set in episcopal rings.

A cross-section of other tourmaline crystals will reveal a green centre surrounded by a pink border. These come from gem-bearing gravels and mines in parts of Africa, such as Mozambique, Angola, Tanzania and Zambia.

THE DUTCH CONNECTION

The Dutch colonists, noting the magnetic quality of tourmaline when it was heated, used long, unfashioned crystals of the gem to draw ash from their tobacco pipes. For this reason they named the stone *ashentrekker* – Ash Puller.

Although tourmaline had been used in the making of jewellery in the Middle and Far East for centuries, it was not until the Dutch introduced the stone into Europe, around the year 1700, that tourmaline became widely known and admired. From about 1750 onward, the

THE Legends ◆ OF TOURMALINE

stone became highly fashionable as a gemstone. As its popularity increased, the common name was changed from *ashentrekker* to the Sinhalese *turmali*.

MAGNETIC AND ELECTRIC

When faces are present on both ends of a natural crystal they can be seen to have developed with different orientations and do not correspond. This phenomenon is known as hemimorphism, and gives the stone certain electrical properties. Tourmaline, for example, is pyroelectric, developing an electrical charge when heated.

This makes it ideal for using in thermometers. Tourmaline also exhibits piezoelecticity, when its crystal are placed under stress. This property is used in underwater detection equipment and in depth and pressure gauges. Another feature of the gem is that, when slices of tourmaline are cut from a prism face, along the length of a crystal, they have the ability to polarize light.

SOME OF THE MANY COLOURS OF TOUR-MALINE ON A SCHIST BACKGROUND

FLINT

*"So stubborn flints their inward heart conceal
Till art and force the unwilling sparks reveal."*

WILLIAM CONGREVE, PLAYWRIGHT (1670-1729)

F lint may seem an unlikely choice for a book such as this, but it has every right to be included as this mineral has been highly prized by many people for centuries. The name flint is a derivative of the Greek word *plinthos*, meaning a brick. Flint is usually found in nodular form, encased in a white crust due to weathering of the nodule surface. It has been described as an impure form of crypto-crystalline chalcedony.

THESE COTTAGES IN NORTHREPP, NEAR CROMER IN NORFOLK, ENGLAND, HAVE BEEN CLAD WITH FLINT. THIS WAS A COMMON PRACTICE IN AREAS WHERE FLINT IS IN PLENTIFUL SUPPLY.

Flint is tough but easily worked – properties that were much valued by Neolithic man, who chipped and formed the stone into all kinds of weapons and tools.

Flint arrowheads (at times known as "glossopetrae") unearthed in the Middle Ages were believed in those times to be the fossilized tongues of serpents, as were the fossil teeth of sharks. These arrowheads and sharks' teeth were often mounted in silver and used as talismans to protect cattle from being bewitched by elves and fairies.

SOLID LIGHTNING

Arrowheads encased in silver came to be regarded as the solid manifestation of lightning flashes, guarding the houses in which they were kept, and those nearby, against being struck by lightning.

In a similar vein, Stone Age flint hammerheads recovered in many parts of

FACT & FANTASY

ANCIENT EGYPTIAN PRIESTS FASHIONED FLINT INTO SPECIAL KNIVES, USED TO MAKE THE FIRST RITUAL INCISION IN A DEAD BODY PRIOR TO EMBALMING. THEY ALSO CARVED FLINT INTO SCARABS – STYLIZED FORMS OF THE LOWLY DUNG BEETLE. THESE SCARABS WERE BELIEVED TO HAVE A SPECIAL INFLUENCE OVER THE HEART, AND WERE WORN AND CARRIED IN THE HOPE THAT THEY WOULD PROTECT THE HEART AND ENABLE ITS OWNER TO ENJOY LONG LIFE.

THE *History* ◆ OF FLINT

THE *Legends* ◆ OF FLINT

Stones. They were considered most effective in protecting people and animals from the ravages of evil spirits, especially the cattle-riding Hag. The stones could also prevent milk from curdling during thunder storms, when these spirits were believed to run riot. Farmers in Eastern Prussia milked their cows in such a way that the milk jetted through a holed flint stone and today some superstitious English dairy farmers still hang such a stone in the dairy.

HEALING FLINT

As long ago as 300 BC, the philosopher Theophrastus recorded many of the healing qualities believed by physicians to be found in this mineral. He writes that, among other powers, flint was credited with the ability to break stones in the kidney and bladder.

During the Middle Ages, any Irish woman fortunate enough to find a flint arrowhead or fossil shark's tooth became elevated to village medical counsellor. Her method of treating people consisted of soaking the arrowhead in water and giving this to the sick person to drink. Horses and cattle wounded by "fairy darts" were also given a similar draught of this healing water. Until recent times, Irish farm workers often wore the *saigead* talisman – an arrowhead set in a silver frame – to protect them from mischievous spells of fairies and elves.

Europe were believed to be a physical manifestation of thunder. Houses, churches and walls built of flintstone can still be seen across large areas of England. Much of this flint may well have originated in the ancient, well-worked mines uncovered in the chalk downs of south and east England.

According to Nordic folklore, flint hammerheads were thrown at misbehaving trolls by Thor, the god of thunder, in an attempt to bring them to order.

HOLEY FLINT

In the north of England, it was the custom to hang a flint with a hole in it around the neck; it might also be tied to the key of the stable door or to the cattle stalls. These stones were called Hag Stones, Holey Stones, Nightmare or Witch Riding

FACT & FANTASY

◆ A TWO-SIDED FLINT BLADE, INFERIOR ACHEULEAN PERIOD (20,000-15,000 BC).

◆ THROUGHOUT THE FIFTEENTH AND SIXTEENTH CENTURIES, A STRONG BELIEF TOOK HOLD THAT FOSSIL GLOSSOPETRAE WERE THE TEETH OF WITCHES AND VAMPIRES WHO PREYED ON THE BLOOD OF INFANTS.

A RANGE OF DISORDERS

As for the holed Hag Stones, they could prevent disorders caused by the Hag sitting on the stomach of a sleeping person, while one placed under the bed was thought to relieve cramp and rheumatism in medieval folk living in the English Midlands. The midwifery folklore of Scandinavia also describes how copious measures of ale are poured over the flint stones and given to the mother-to-be to drink, to ensure an easy birth.

OPAL

Grey years ago a man lived in the East,

Who did possess a ring of worth immense

From a beloved hand. Opal the stone,

Which flashed a hundred bright

  and beauteous hues,

And had the power to make beloved

of God, and Man the blessed and fortunate.

LESSING, IN HIS BOOK *NATHAN THE WISE*

Too much pressure can cause cracks to occur.

These mishaps seem to have given rise in some quarters to the idea that opals are unlucky, although they are generally seen as bringing good fortune to those who take good care of them.

Hyalite, generally known as Water Opal, is completely clear but shows a good, sometimes spectacular, play of colour. The variety called Hydrophane offers no play of colour until immersed in water or oil. Fire Opal is a transparent or semi-transparent stone of a red or orange tint, which may or may not have a play of colour.

The beautiful play of colours across the opal is produced by the way in which light is affected by the gem's three-dimensional lattice, which in turn is made up of tiny spheres of amorphous silica, rather than a regular pattern of crystals.

A DELICATE STONE

The stone forms from a silica jelly which has solidified yet retains a small amount of water; in some cases this can amount to about 10 per cent of its body weight. Opals are delicate and too much warmth may evaporate some of their water content and cause them to lose their lustre. Also, moving from a hot room to the cold of outdoors may sometimes craze the surface of a polished opal, while

THE *History* ◆ OF OPAL

THE Legends ◆ OF OPAL

FAVOURITE OF THE ANCIENTS

Opal's ancient Greek name was *paederos*, and the derivation of this meant both "child" and "favourite" – inferring that it had the same kind of peerless beauty as a child.

The Romans also gave the name *paederos* to opal, as well as to amethyst and to two species of plant. Pliny wrote of the play of colour:

"There is in them a softer fire than in the carbuncle; there is the brilliant purple of the amethyst; there is the sea green of the emerald – all shining together in incredible union."

LIKE THE REST OF HIS COUNTRYMEN, MARK ANTONY VALUED THE OPAL VERY HIGHLY, BANISHING A SENATOR WHO REFUSED TO GIVE UP HIS PRIZE STONE

The Romans eagerly sought to possess any opal, as it was considered to bring good fortune. So much so that, when Senator Nonius refused to give up his opal to Mark Anthony, the latter outlawed the senator.

THE MIDDLE AGES

During the Middle Ages, the Hungarian opal mines in Czernowitz (Chernovtsy) were very active and more than three hundred miners were employed during the mid-fifteenth century. Over the span of the mine's life, and right up to the mid-eighteenth century, opals continued to be sought after as attractive talismans.

When it was announced that opal deposits had been discovered in Australia, Queen Victoria of England was delighted. Her Majesty commissioned the Royal jewellers to make her many pieces of opal jewellery – and the gem returned to favour.

OPAL OF THE EMPERORS

Legend tells of a dazzling gemstone set into the crown of the Holy Roman Emperors, which was reputed to watch over the royal family. The gem was believed to have been a magnificent opal and Albertus Magnus (1193–1280), one-time Bishop of Ratisbon, claimed that:

"None like it has ever been seen... Its hue is as though pure white snow flashed and sparkled with the colour of bright, ruddy wine... It is a translucent stone, and there is a tradition that it formerly shone in the night-time."

He goes on to say that it cured eye diseases and could "render its wearer invisible, and therefore it was called Patronus Furum – Patron of Thieves."

In common with many gems, the opal was believed to shield the wearer from contagion, and to warn of the presence of poison by losing its play of colour. It was worn as a pendant to dispel melancholia, while an opal necklace was worn by those who wanted their hair to remain blonde.

SPECIMENS OF OPAL FROM AUSTRALIA. SHOWN HERE IS A SAMPLE OF CRAGGY OPAL MATRIX FROM QUEENSLAND, AN OPAL CAMEO AND TWO DOUBLET STONES

MOONSTONE

"It is a very powerful stone in the reconciling of love, and during the whole time of the increase of the moon, it helps the pthisical (consumptive); but in the decrease it discovers surprising effects, for it enables a person to foretell future events."

CAMILLUS LEONARDUS,
SIXTEENTH-CENTURY PHYSICIAN

Moonstone is a type of feldspar known as orthoclase, with a monoclinic crystal system. Recovered from mines in Sri-Lanka, Switzerland and Burma, the mineral has "cleavage planes" that produce a silvery bluish-white chatoyancy – an almost cat's eye quality that changes in relation to the light reflected from its surface.

A REFLECTION OF THE MOON

Pliny mentions stones called astrion, astriotes and ceraunia, and these were very probably what we now know as moonstone. He describes the first two as being transparent, like rock crystal, but with a bright white spot that appears to move as the stone is rotated and twisted in the fingers. This spot was believed by the ancients to be a reflection of the moon – Pliny compares astrion and astriotes with "a star shining brightly like the full moon" – and the bright spot was thought to wax and wane in harmony with lunar movement.

According to Pliny, astrion and astriotes were so-named because, when held up to the stars, the stones collected and reflected their glitter. Pliny: "The best

THE *History* ◆ OF MOONSTONE

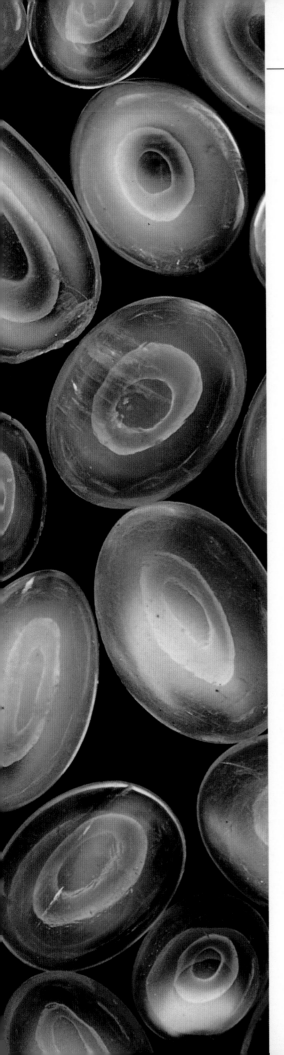

THE *Legends*
◆ OF MOONSTONE

kind came from Carmania and were called 'ceraunia' (thunder stones). They imprison a bright star, and although in itself it is like rock crystal, has a brilliant blue sheen." He also spoke of dull ceraunia stones which "if steeped in soda and vinegar for several days form such a star which fades away after several months."

SELENITES STONES

Camillus Leonardus lists the stone as selenites. It contains, he says, the figure of the moon or a clouded star and claimed that samples from Persia increase or decrease in colour in time with the phases of the moon. He continues:

"Being put in the mouth, which must first be washed with water, such affairs are thought of as ought or ought not to be taken in hand. If to be undertaken, they are so fixed in the mind that they cannot be forgotten but if not, they soon vanish out of the mind."

ONCE IN A BLUE MOON

On the Asian continent, the pale lustrous blue colour of the moonstone is considered to resemble moonlight. However, the best of the blue moonstones are washed up by the tides when the Sun and the Moon are in a particular heavenly and harmonious relationship, which occurs every twenty one years (three 7-year cycles of the moon). This event gives rise to the saying that denotes a lengthy period of time – "Once in a Blue Moon".

• •

SINCE EARLIEST TIMES, THE STONE HAS BEEN ASSOCIATED WITH THE VERY SPECIAL LIGHT OF THE MOON

• •

THE RAINBOW HUES OF THE TYPICAL MOONSTONE ARE CAUSED BY CLEAVAGE PLANES IN THE MINERAL

ROCK CRYSTAL

"Why it is formed with hexagonal faces cannot readily be explained: and any explanation is complicated by the fact that, on the one hand, its terminal points are not symmetrical, and that on the other, its faces are so perfectly smooth that no craftsmanship could achieve the same effect."

PLINY, IN *HISTORIA NATURALIS*

The ancients had a theory about crystal formation based on the idea that crystals were actually made of ice, formed in remote, freezing places (see pages 16-17). What they were thinking about principally when they spoke of this was later found to be just one specific type of mineral, quartz, especially the clear and colourless form. Clear quartz is now called rock crystal.

Quartz is silicon dioxide and it is one of the commonest minerals on the face of the globe, making up about 60 per cent of the Earth's crust. All the world's golden, sandy beaches are actually composed of tiny crystals of quartz, stained gold by water-borne iron. The colour of the quartz depends on which transition elements have been at work and it comes in many varieties, including:

- amethyst (purple); see pages 62-65
- rose quartz (pink)
- citrine (yellow)
- rock crystal (colourless)

THE *History* OF ROCK CRYSTAL

A SAMPLE OF RUTILATED QUARTZ, FOUND IN BAHIA, BRAZIL

Rock crystal is the most widespread quartz variety. Their crystals, which form in the trigonal system, have an unusual helical pattern that spirals either to the left or to the right.

Flawless crystals like clear water were known to the Greeks as *acenteta* or "without a core". These crystals were considered things of great beauty and were left un-engraved and unworked. And as for the Romans, they imported large quantities of rock crystal from Alabandina in Asia Minor, and the ice theory prompted fashionable ladies to carry spheres of crystal in their hands to cool them during summer weather.

SPECIAL PROPERTIES

Today, rock crystal has some very different uses. The natural crystal is both pyroelectric and piezoelectric. This means that, when the crystal is subjected to heat, an electric charge is generated on its surface; an electric current is also generated when the crystal is subjected to strain. Conversely, applying an electric current to this mineral actually causes strains in the crystals. The same phenomena occur in synthetic quartz.

These important physical properties have been exploited in various ways for many years. Quartz is used in the depth-measuring instruments needed for deep sea diving. The great pressure generated at vast depths causes quartz crystals to "energize" special meters, which then record either the depth or the pressure. In the same way, rock crystal can provide the spark that makes a cigarette lighter work, or lights a gas cooker.

TIME-KEEPING

As for time-keeping, small batteries delivering an electric current induce rapid vibrations in the crystals fitted in quartz analogue clocks and watches. These vibrations are counted by a tiny computer chip, which allows the necessary number of vibrations through to move the clock mechanism. This piezoelectric effect is also used in the generation and control of radio frequencies.

THE *Legends* ◆ OF ROCK CRYSTAL

THE SOLDIERS' FRIEND

According to Pliny, Roman armies used spheres and lenses fashioned from rock crystal to focus the rays of the Sun whenever there was a need to cauterize severe wounds suffered by their soldiers during battle.

For many centuries, rock crystal beads were made into necklaces that were believed to ensure copious supplies of milk from nursing mothers. It also worked its charms on the animal kingdom, relieving disease in cattle. According to Dr William T. Fernie, writing during the 1800s, powdered rock crystal suspended in wine was administered in the treatment of dysentery and transparent quartz crystals were used to reduce the heat of fevers and slake the feverish thirst.

MAGICIANS, TALISMANS AND SEERS

The story of those who foretell the future by gazing into crystal balls is a long one. From the fifth century onwards, these crystals were usually made of beryl, but by the mid-nineteenth century, rock crystal spheres had taken their place (by the turn of the century they would be made of glass).

Native Australian medicine men claim that rock crystal pebbles, known as "ultunda stones", are embedded in their bodies and ensure personal magical powers for as long as they remain there. According to *The Handbook of American Indians North of Mexico* (1910), rock crystal came to be regarded as a powerful hunting talisman. It was considered a living entity that required feeding – by rubbing the crystal in the blood of fallen prey.

FACT & FANTASY

◆ THE WORLD'S LARGEST CRYSTAL BALL WAS CUT IN CHINA FROM BURMESE ROCK CRYSTAL. IT HAD A DIAMETER OF OVER 30 CM.

◆ THE SMITHSONIAN INSTITUTE IN AMERICA HAS ON DISPLAY A ROCK CRYSTAL SPHERE OF NEARLY THE SAME SIZE.

◆ AN AWE-INSPIRING EXAMPLE OF AZTEC WORKMANSHIP SURVIVES IN A ROCK CRYSTAL SKULL THAT MEASURES ABOUT 20 CM ACROSS ITS WIDTH.

◆ IN PARTS OF ASIA, ROCK CRYSTAL IS THOUGHT TO BE AN UNRIPE DIAMOND.

ZIRCON

"It raises men to noble honours and preserves from epidemical distempers."

CAMILLUS LEONARDUS,
SIXTEENTH-CENTURY PHYSICIAN

TRAVELLERS, SUCH AS THE CRUSADERS, CARRIED ZIRCON AS A TALISMAN
....

This mineral is a silicate of zirconium, and it forms in the tetragonal crystal system. In one particular type of zircon, called Low Zircon, the crystalline structure has broken down over millions of years and it is now almost an amorphous body. This is caused by radiation coming from particles of uranium trapped within the zircon, or found nearby, during the stone's formation. Zircon is found in Sri Lanka, Burma, Thailand, South West Africa, Australia, France, the USA and Canada.

There seems to be some doubt as to whether the modern zircon stone was the zircon known to the ancients. For instance, lapis hyacinthus, according to

During the Crusades, and for many centuries afterwards, "jargoon" was the word that was used to describe all zircon stones in the colourless to pale yellow range. "Hyacinth" (or jacinth), on the other hand, was used for zircon of an orange to reddish colour. Expertise was so lacking in the identification of gemstones that hessonite garnet was also numbered among stones mistakenly identified as hyacinth.

The name jacinth is of Arabic origin, although hyacinth is deeply rooted in Greek legend. According to this legend, the stone's colour is identical to that of the flower that Apollo caused to grow from the blood of Hyacinthus, whom he had accidentally killed.

FACT & FANTASY

CERTAIN UNSCRUPULOUS "GEM COOKS" HEAT THE BROWNISH RED CRYSTALS OF ZIRCON TO PRODUCE IMITATIONS OF OTHER GEMS. IT IS DIFFICULT TO CONTROL WHICH COLOUR WILL EMERGE FROM HEATING A PARTICULAR BATCH, BUT GOOD COLOURLESS RESULTS HAVE BEEN PASSED OFF AS DIAMONDS BY UNSCRUPULOUS DEALERS – COLOURLESS ZIRCON ACTUALLY HAS A GREATER FIRE THAN ANY OTHER KNOWN GEM EXCEPT THE DIAMOND. CUT AND POLISHED CLEAR ZIRCON IS OFTEN KNOWN AS "MATURA DIAMOND".

HEATING ZIRCON IN A CRUCIBLE, TOGETHER WITH CHARCOAL, CAUSES THEM TO ASSUME A STRIKINGLY BEAUTIFUL BLUE COLOUR. THESE ATTRACTIVE STONES ARE GIVEN THE NAME "STARLIGHT".

THE *History* OF ZIRCON

THE *Legends*
◆ OF ZIRCON

Pliny, had the violet radiance of the amethyst "diluted with the tint of the hyacinth flower." The blue stones that he was referring to may actually have been blue corundum (sapphires).

In the modern age, zircon has been prized as an inexpensive diamond look-alike with various other applications. Around 1886, for example, the demand for zircon increased rapidly as it was then used in certain kinds of gas burners.

LEGENDS AND STORIES

Within the Latin verse penned by Marbodus is the suggestion that jacinth makes people agreeable and attractive, and Camillus Leonardus tells us that this stone "invigorates animal life, especially the heart, and increases ingenuity, glory and riches."

Paracelsus the Great (1493–1541) recommended powdered jacinth, mixed with laudanum, as a remedy for fevers resulting from "putrifaction of the air or water", while Francesco India, a renowned sixteenth-century Veronese physician, was not convinced by the effects of powdered gemstones, but

believed that wearing a jacinth over the heart strengthened that organ considerably. Another declared that "jacinth forecast an impending tempest when it assumed the hue of burning coal" and "lost its colour when worn by anyone suffering from the plague".

BELOVED OF GOD

According to Konrad von Megenberg (*Book of Nature*, 1861), citing Thomas de Cantimpre, the stone had the virtue of making the wearer "beloved of God and men." It protected the wearer from melancholia and poison, and relieved indigestion, jaundice, dropsy and all manner of fevers. Jacinth also acted as a barometer – the imminent onset of bad weather caused the stone to become cloudy and dull, but the stone brightened magnificently when forecasting a fine, sunny day.

Anselmus Boetius de Boot (*Gemmarum et Lapidum*, 1636) recommended the wearing of a jacinth set in gold to bring sleep to the insomniac, but Leonardus recorded a warning by Aristotle that the gem "prepared a woman for miscarriage."

MERCHANTS AND TRAVELLERS

Whether at home or abroad, merchants carried this stone as their talisman, believing that its magical powers protected them from lightning and defended them against enemies and bandits. Leonardus recorded the stone as giving security to travellers in that "no pestilence in any country shall hurt them; it raises men to noble honours and preserves them from epidemical distempers."

NATURAL BROWN ZIRCON CRYSTALS FORM IN THE TETRAGONAL SYSTEM

DIAMOND

"Better a diamond with a flaw than a pebble without."

CONFUCIOUS

To most people, this is the finest gemstone of them all – and we have been amazed by its properties and beauties since earliest times. For its unsurpassed hardness – diamond is right at the apex of Moh's Scale (see page 10) – the Greeks gave the name *adamas* to this mineral, which means "hard" and "untameable".

Many have written of diamonds: the great Roman scholar Pliny also observed the extraordinary hardness of this remarkable mineral. In his writings he maintained that steeping diamonds in warm, fresh goat's blood helped to soften them although, even then, they "may break all but the best anvils and iron hammers".

He goes on to say that, if finally broken, diamond shatters into splinters that "are much sought after by engravers of gems and are inserted by them into iron tools because they make hollows in the hardest materials without difficulty."

**BEAUTIFUL, HARD AND RARE –
DIAMOND IS THE ULITMATE GEM**

FORMING CLOSE BONDS

Diamond is made of carbon, and the carbon atoms in this gemstone are very firmly and closely bonded together, giving it a tightly knit, extremely hard structure. There are, of course, weaknesses in the bonds between the atoms in certain directions, and these enable diamond to be cleaved or split – but only along specific cleavage planes. Clever use of these cleavage planes enables the lapidary to shape a rough diamond into a form with the very best weight and shape.

Scientists have a comprehensive knowledge of the material that forms diamond, and the necessary temperatures and pressures required to transform a graphite form of carbon to diamond. At the present time, however, we have no absolute knowledge of the origins of this fabulous gemstone.

Some researchers believe that the carbon atoms that make up diamond are liberated from gasses generated within magma chambers in the Earth's mantle, and are then are carried towards each other by the action of convection currents in the magma (see page 8). The magma then becomes the "mother liquor" in which the diamonds grow.

KIMBERLITE

Under the vast pressures and temperatures of the mantle, magma sometimes finds a small crack in the Earth's crust through which it squeezes – like toothpaste from its tube. As the magma cools, diamond and other gem crystals are formed and are brought to the surface of the Earth along with the magma. At this point, the magma becomes what diamond miners call kimberlite, named after the town of Kimberley (near Johannesburg, South Africa) where prospectors first dug for diamonds. Millions of years ago, great pipes of kimberlite reached thousands of metres in height.

DIAMOND CRYSTALS

Diamonds form in the cubic crystal system, but they are rarely found as cubes. The usual form is octahedral (two four-sided pyramids, base to base). Others are found as dodecahedrons (twelve lozenge-shaped faces) and as icositetrahedrons (24 kite-shaped faces).

Sometimes the octahedral faces are replaced by three- or six-faced pyramids, while many crystals are found in misshapen forms such as triangles, dog tooth shapes, elongated dodecahedra and so on.

SEEING THE LIGHT

One of the main things that gives diamonds such beauty is their fabulous fire and sparkle. The quality of the gem's lustre (termed "adamantine"), which is unique to diamond, is dependent on the quality and quantity of light reflected from its surface (around 17 per cent) and reflected from inside the stone (around 80 per cent).

In the cutting and shaping of a round "brilliant" there are three important components:

1. The table – the main central facet on the top of the gem;
2. The crown facets – the facets around the table, at the top of the gem;
3. The pavilion facets – long facets at the stone's underside

Light entering through the table is totally reflected out of the stone by the pavilion facets. Some passes through the table; some through the crown facets. The facet angles that give maximum sparkle have been carefully calculated by scientists – for example, it is the angle at which light hits the crown facets that gives a diamond its famous fire. The shape and proportions of the stone are also important factors.

The polished, cut diamond is like a prism, so that rays of light entering the stone become separated out according to their wavelengths. The longer red rays are bent the least; the shorter violet rays are bent the most. This separation of white light into its seven component colours is called dispersion.

Some of the internally reflected light of a diamond leaves through the crown facets, providing prismatic flashes of colour – the "fire" of the stone. Green demantoid garnet and zircon are the only natural gemstones whose surface lustre and fire approaches that of diamond.

....

THREE DIAMOND CRYSTALS FLUORESC-ING UNDER ULTRAVIOLET LIGHT

**DIAMOND RINGS WERE VERY POPULAR
DURING THE REIGN OF ELIZABETH I**
....

During the Middle Ages, diamonds were the knight's talisman and those who could obtain the stones had them set into their armour, shields and sword hilts in the hope that this gem would protect them and bring victory. The stones, mostly from India, were mounted in the knights' armour in the same rough condition as they had been found.

Several centuries were to pass before Indian diamond miners discovered a way to polish a table on to the stone. As a consequence, diamonds did not really become "a girl's best friend" until the beautiful Agnes Sorel became the first "commoner" to wear a diamond necklace.

Agnes was the beautiful mistress of Charles VII of France, and she became acquainted with a wealthy merchant called Jacques Coeur. Charles was running out of funds to continue his war with the English, and Agnes asked Jacques to lend the King sufficient funds to pay his army. As a reward, Jaques was appointed financial adviser to the King and Agnes then persuaded Charles to make him Master of the Royal Mint.

Grateful Jacques paid his debt to Agnes with a few diamonds, skilfully cut and set as jewels by the finest goldsmiths. And so the lovely Agnes became the first commoner to wear diamonds and the first European to wear a diamond necklace.

ROYAL RINGS

For a long time, it was a tradition for European royalty to give rings as rewards for services rendered and many wore large numbers of rings on each hand. The English king Henry VIII sported rings on every finger, including the thumb, and an effigy of El Cid, lying in Escorial Monastery, just beyond Madrid, shows many rings decorating each hand.

During the reign of Elizabeth I of England, there arose a craze for "scribbling rings", fashioned by inserting a diamond octahedron – one point uppermost – into a heavy gold ring. Using the point of the diamond, Elizabethan dandies would scribble sweet nothings on the windows of whichever lady had caught their eye.

A well-recorded anecdote tells of Sir Walter Raleigh scribbling on Elizabeth's window: "Fain would I rise but that I fear to fall." The Queen replied: "If thy heart fail thee, do not rise at all."

FACE-POLISHING

Very small quantities of diamonds were available at this time. Sometimes they were natural crystals of diamond that required no polishing because the stones were as transparent as glass; today's diamond traders call these stones "glassies".

FACT & FANTASY

UNTIL THE EIGHTEENTH CENTURY, MOST DIAMONDS CAME FROM INDIA AND WERE TRADED FOR FROM AS EARLY AS 800 BC. THESE INDIAN STONES WERE RECOVERED FROM ALLUVIAL DEPOSITS, ALONG WITH GOLD, RUBY, SAPPHIRE AND GARNET. THEY WERE NOT RECOVERED FROM KIMBERLITE PIPES, AS IS THE GREATER PROPORTION OF DIAMONDS RECOVERED IN OTHER PARTS OF THE WORLD TODAY.

ACCORDING TO S. M. TAGORE (1879), THE FRENCH TRADER AND EXPLORER TAVERNIER VISITED THREE DIAMOND MINES IN INDIA. TAVERNIER GIVES A VIVID DESCRIPTION OF ONE MINE, SAYING THAT THE MEN WERE EMPLOYED TO DIG, "AND THE WOMEN AND CHILDREN TO CARRY THE EARTH."

THE *History*
◆ OF DIAMONDS

Around 1500, the table cut had been joined, and would eventually be replaced, by a new style. This was the rose cut, a most useful style of cut when polishing thin, flat stones. Many rose cut stones were foiled (enclosed) at the back with a suitably faceted gold plate. This practice enabled skilful jewellers to make very impressive pieces of jewellery.

THE PEACOCK THRONE

From 1631, the French explorer Tavernier made six incursions into the Far East. He brought home great riches in diamond and other precious gemstones: gems collected from the palaces of the Great Moguls and lesser rulers.

He also told tales of many extraordinary gems in his *The Six Voyages of J. B. Tavernier*, published in 1676.

For example, his description of the splendid Peacock Throne, at the court in Delhi, included the following:

"The underpart of the canopy is all embroidered with pearls and diamonds. On the top stands a Peacock with his tail spread, consisting of sapphires and other stones... When the King seats himself upon the throne there is a transparent jewel with a diamond appendant of about 80 or 90 carats encompassed with rubies and emeralds, so hung that it is always in his eye... Upon each side of the throne are two parasols, the handles covered with diamonds."

BRAZILIAN DIAMONDS

Two main factors boosted the availability of diamonds:

• Vasco de Gama had discovered a new sea route to India

• as a result of this, production at the Indian mines was increased.

India continued to enjoy its position as the leading diamond producer until about 1728, when diamonds were discovered in Brazil.

....

CLOCKWISE FROM TOP LEFT: DIAMONDS IN CONGLOMERATE, FROM NAMAQUALAND; IN KIMBERLITE FROM S. AFRICA; IN MATRIX FROM SIBERIA

**COLOURED DIAMOND CRYSTALS
STAND OUT VIVIDLY AGAINST A
BACKGROUND OF JET**
·······························

Possession of a diamond was said to give its owner immunity from scourges such as the plague. It also granted absolute freedom from demons and devils, taming the dreaded incubii and sucubii who rode their victims roughly across the countryside in the dead of night. It was diamond's power to ward off evil that led people to start exchanging diamond betrothal rings, especially as the fashion for exchanging jewelled rings as tokens of affection was well established by the sixteenth century.

THE VALLEY OF DIAMONDS

A treatise on mineralogy by Al Kazwani, an Arabian philosopher of the ninth century, claims that the philosopher Aristotle told the following story:

"Other than my pupil Alexander, no one has ever reached the valley where the diamonds are found. It lies in the East, along the great border of Khurasan, and this valley is connected with the land of Hind.

"The glance cannot penetrate to its greatest depths and serpents are found there the like of which no man hath seen, and upon which no man can gaze without dying... Now, Alexander ordered that an iron mirror be brought and placed at the spot where the serpents dwelt; and when the serpents approached, their glance fell upon their own image in the mirror, and this caused their death."

"Hereupon Alexander wished to bring out the diamonds in the valley, but no one was willing to make the descent. Alexander therefore consulted his school of wise men, who advised him to have pieces of flesh thrown into the valley. This he ordered to be done, and so the diamonds became attached to the flesh and the birds of the air seized the flesh and bore it up out of the valley. Then Alexander ordered his people to pursue the birds and pick up what fell from the flesh."

A THOUSAND AND ONE TALES

Over the following centuries, all kinds of stories about this magical valley cropped up. The legend appeared in one of the tales told in *A Thousand and One Nights* – a collection of stories told by the beautiful Scheherazade to divert a mighty Arabian king and keep him from killing her.

In Scheherazade's tale, an adventurous sailor called Sinbad is dropped from the claws of a giant bird into an inaccessible valley. The floor of this valley is covered with diamonds and poisonous snakes and the sailor fills his pockets with gems before being lifted to safety by another giant bird.

Legends
OF DIAMONDS

MARCO POLO

Marco Polo also recounts the legend of the valley in his *Travels*. He tells us that the valley is in the kingdom of "Motupali", which was ruled by queen Rudrama Devi until around 1295. It has been established that these diamond mines are at Golconda, in Hyderabad.

He also tells us that there are many mountains in which the diamonds are found:

"When it rains, the water rushes down through the mountains, scouring its way through mighty gorges and caverns. When the rain has stopped and the water has drained away, then the men go in search of diamond through these gorges from which the water has come, and they find plenty. Moreover, the mountains are so infested with serpents of immense size and girth that men cannot go there without grave danger."

He goes on to describe a deep, serpent-filled valley with walls

that men fear to enter. Great eagles preyed on the poisonous serpents. Recovery of the diamonds is achieved in the way described by Aristotle – by throwing haunches of raw meat into the valley – although they were also found in the droppings of the eagles.

Some researchers believe that the Valley of Diamonds is situated somewhere in the mountains of Serendib (Sri Lanka), but the exact location has been long-lost.

PRECIOUS MEDICINE

Those physicians who had care of Pope Clement VII, sometime in 1532, prescribed costly doses of various powdered precious stones – mostly diamond powder. Spaniards were prolific users of diamond dust to treat the plague and ailments of the bladder.

Hindu physicians were convinced that diamond powder produced from unflawed stones, and taken internally, guaranteed strength, energy, beauty, a clear skin, happiness, longevity and a continuous sense of well-being. On the other hand, powder produced from flawed diamond generated every illness from lameness to psoriasis.

WELL-CUT DIAMONDS MAKE THE MOST OF THE STONE'S INCREDIBLE "FIRE"

THE KOH-I-NOOR

At the time of Shah Jehan, around 1600, an important diamond was in the possession of the Mogul Dynasty. This was a great stone to which various superstitions had become attached. The Moguls believed that he who owned this stone would rule the world, and it had been set as one of the eyes in the peacock of the Peacock Throne (in the palace at Delhi). It was Shah Jehan who built the beautiful, much-jewelled Taj Mahal palace, in memory of his lovely wife, Mumtaz.

When, in 1739, Persia's Nadir Shah invaded India and pillaged the city of Delhi, he was unable to find the great diamond but he received intelligence that Mohammed Shah – the defeated Mogul ruler – had secreted the gemstone in his turban.

INVITATION TO THE FEAST

To gain possession of the coveted stone, Nadir took advantage of an ancient Asian custom by inviting Mohammed to a feast at which it was suggested that turbans were exchanged. Nadir retired from the feast and, as he unwound the turban and the glittering prize fell to the floor, he exclaimed "Koh-i-Noor", which means "Mountain of Light". And so the stone was named.

The great stone would make many more journeys over the following years,

until it was presented to Queen Victoria in 1850. By this time it was said to bring great misfortune to any man who wore it, but not to a woman. This was taken seriously by Queen Victoria, and is said to have made her add a clause to her will stating that, when the diamond came to be inherited by a male sovereign, it was only to be worn by his queen.

To this day the Koh-i-Noor has been set only in the crowns of Queen Alexandria, Queen Mary, and, in 1936, the crown of Queen Elizabeth, the British Queen Mother.

THE SANCY

The Sancy, or to give it its full title, Le Grand Sancy, is a pear-shaped diamond weighing 55 carats. It is claimed to be one of the earliest stones that was cut and polished with symmetrical facets.

The stone was purchased in around 1570 by Nicholas Harlai, Seigneur de Sancy in Constantinople, where he was stationed as French Ambassador to Turkey; the stone was eventually named after him.

On his return to France, he took the stone with him, where its existence came to the attention of the French king, Henry III of France. The king

was very sensitive about his baldness and always wore a small velvet cap. To decorate his cap he "borrowed" the stone from Sancy.

VALUABLE SECURITY

Henry IV eventually promoted Sancy as his Superintendent of Finance, asking

THE Legends OF DIAMONDS

DIAMOND FABLES
ARE AS FABULOUS AS
THE STONE ITSELF

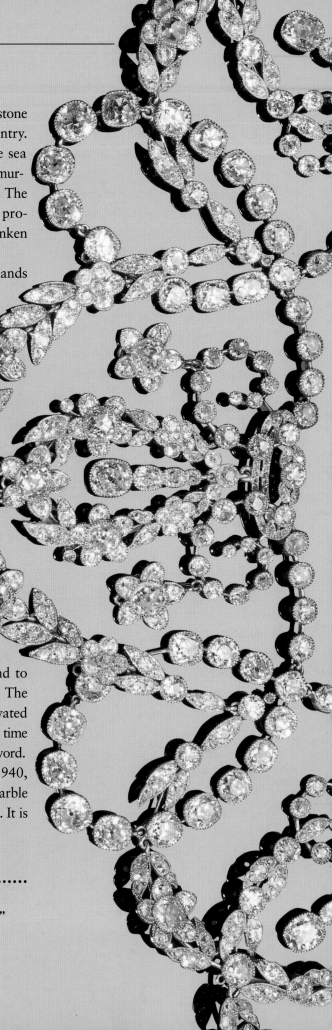

and bartering half the value of the stone for a sea passage to another country. Once well out into the ocean, the sea captain who had accepted the deal murdered the slave and stole the stone. The story goes that he squandered the proceeds on liquor and, in a fit of drunken remorse, hanged himself.

After passing through several hands the stone was bought by Thomas Pitt, Governor of Madras and grandfather of William Pitt, who became prime minister of Britain. William sent the stone to England, where diamond cutters took two years to fashion it into a 140-carat cushion shape.

The Duke of Orleans, Regent of France, purchased the Pitt diamond in 1717. As a result, the name of the stone was changed to "The Regent".

At his coronation in 1722, Louis XIV had the Regent set as a feature in his crown and Marie Antoinette is reported to have used the diamond to decorate a large black velvet hat. The Regent then stayed within elevated French circles for many years, at one time decorating Napoleon's coronation sword.

When Hitler invaded Paris in 1940, the Regent was hidden behind a marble fireplace in the Chateau Chambord. It is now on display in the Louvre.

••••••••••••••••••••••••••••••••••••••
A DIAMOND CHOKER NECKLACE , DATING FROM THE "BELLE EPOQUE" ERA, JUST BEFORE WORLD WAR I

him to lend the diamond as security for the raising of money to pay the army.

A messenger was dispatched with the diamond, but the messenger never reached the king, and his body was found some time later, hidden in a hedge, horribly mutilated. According to local legend, the diamond was recovered from the stomach of the messenger, who had swallowed it for safe keeping.

Since then, the stone passed between several owners before being bought by the Astor family.

THE REGENT

The story of this stone begins about 1701, when it was found by an Indian slave working at the Parteal mine, on the River Kistna. It weighed 410 carats and was one of the last large diamonds to be found in India.

The slave is supposed to have hidden this great diamond in a self-inflicted leg wound before escaping from the mine

THE FLORENTINE

This was the stone once possessed by Charles the Bold, Duke of Burgundy, and also owned at one time by the powerful Medici family. A legend tells of the stone being lost on the field of battle when Charles' army was defeated, in 1477. This diamond, together with a large pearl, was found in a small silver box lying, apparently abandoned, on the battlefield. The soldier who found the box is said to have sold the diamond and the pearl to the priest of a nearby village.

The stone's first authentic record was made by the explorer Tavernier in 1657, when he saw it among the treasures of the Grand Duke of Tuscany. He describes it as a diamond of a citron yellow colour. In due time, the stone passed to Francis Stephan of Lorraine (Duke of Tuscany) and then to the Austrian Royal House when he married Empress Marie Theresa, in 1736. The Florentine was later set in the Hapsburg Crown.

INTO EXILE

After the fall of the Austrian Empire, the stone was taken by the Austrian Royal Family to Switzerland, where they went to live in exile. It is thought to have been stolen from their keeping and sold in South America, together with other Crown gems. The diamond was cut as a double rose, with nine irregular sides. It weighed 137.27 carats and had 126 polished facets.

At the beginning of World War II, the German army invaded Austria and was reported to have carried off the Florentine. If this was so, it can only have been a replica – if the story surrounding the Emperor's exile is true.

THE HOPE

In 1668, Tavernier was presented to King Louis XIV, who expressed a wish to see his fantastic collection of diamonds. Among the many stones shown to the King was a blue stone weighing 112

THE ANCIENTS OFTEN GROUPED COLOURLESS STONES, BUT DIAMONDS ARE IN A CLASS OF THEIR OWN

carats. The King purchased 22 diamonds, including the "blue", and this strikingly coloured stone became officially known as "The Blue Diamond of the Crown".

The stone had been cut by Indian lapidaries to give maximum weight, but

THE Legends
◆ OF DIAMONDS

the King ordered it to be re-cut to give maximum brilliance and, in doing so, reduced the weight of this magnificent stone to 67.50 carats.

The stone was among those stolen during the French Revolution and it has never been recovered. However, some experts believe that the Hope Diamond was cut from the famous Blue stone.

BAD FORTUNE

The Hope takes its name from its one-time owner, a banker and gem-collector called Henry Phillip Hope, who purchased the stone for $90,000 in 1830. The stone acquired its reputation for visiting bad luck on its owner while it was in the possession of the Hope family – Phillip's nephew, Thomas Henry Hope, lost his fortune after inheriting the stone.

Abdul Hamid II, a Turkish Sultan, purchased the stone in 1908. He is numbered among those who suffered from its supposedly malignant influence, as there is a reference to his near death shortly after facing a revolution and losing his Sultanate. He placed the stone on the open market and Mrs Edward B. McLean – wife of the owner of the *Washington Post* – came into possession of the Hope in 1911.

Despite the many legends of violent deaths and disasters surrounding the diamond, Mrs McLean never considered selling the stone or believed that a piece

of inert material could exert such a malign influence – even though her only son was killed in an accident. Nor did that belief waver when later she lost her personal fortune.

FACT & FANTASY

◆ A FABULOUS DIAMOND WITH MYSTI-CAL SIGNIFICANCE: THE KOH-I-NOOR NOW RESIDES IN THE CROWN OF QUEEN ELIZABETH, THE BRITISH QUEEN MOTHER.

◆ DIAMONDS SUCH AS THE HOPE ARE COLOURED BY THE ELEMENT BORON. MOST BLUE DIAMONDS ARE INERT UNDER LONG WAVE UV LIGHT AND SHOW A BLUE FLUORESCENCE UNDER SHORT WAVE UV. BUT THE HOPE IS EXCEPTIONAL – WHEN SHORT WAVE UV STIMULATION IS REMOVED, IT GLOWS RED LIKE A HOT COAL.

2

Organic GEMS

"It is intriguing to realize that the trees whose lifeblood became today's amber were living organisms more than fifty million years before the first human beings walked on this earth. What our limited vision calls 'antiquity'... seems quite modern by comparison with the antiquity of a piece of amber."

BARBARA G. WALKER, IN
THE BOOK OF SACRED STONES

While the majority of gemstones are mineral and so inorganic in origin, the organic world also has all kinds of beautiful gems to offer. Some of the most stunning and prized stones originate in the plant or animal world – from the rich golden hues of amber, encasing the fascinating remains of life forms from many millions of years ago, to the lovely delicacy of coral (shown on the right) and the cool, simple beauty of the pearl.

AMBER

"Pretty in amber to observe the forms

Of hairs, or straws, or dirt, or grubs, or worms!

The things, we know, are neither rich or rare,

But wonder how the devil they got there."

ALEXANDER POPE, POET (1688–1744)

Although amber is characteristically a golden orange hue, other colours of amber are also found. These rarer colours are violet, orange, yellow, green, blue and even black. Carvings in these hues are much sought after by collectors, blues and greens being the most valuable.

Amber may be transparent or translucent and has a greasy shine. Air spaces inside the amber give it a cloudy appearance; heating the amber in oil fills the spaces and makes it transparent.

WHAT IS AMBER?

Amber is the fossilized resin of trees. Insects, pieces of moss, lichens and pine needles may be found in amber, having been trapped millions of years ago while the resin was still sticky. Despite its origins, however, amber has just the same attributes of beauty, rarity and durability as mineral gems.

Over the centuries, philosophers and alchemists conjured up delightful but fanciful theories to explain the origins of amber. In ancient Rome, Demonstratus, a first-century AD Roman senator and historian, records in his manuscripts a popular belief that amber was formed from the urine of the lynx: tawny, dark sherry colours being the product of the male, and lighter coloured ambers produced by the female lynx.

Another ancient belief holds that the rays of a brilliantly setting sun became congealed in an evening sea and were cast upon the shore in the form of amber.

However, in about 240 BC, Sudines, an astrologer who lived at the court of Attalus I of Pergamum, wrote a treatise on the mystical properties of gemstones. He wrote that amber is the product of a tree that grows in Liguria, a tree known as the "lynx".

TYPES OF AMBER

Gemmologists divide amber into four groups:

1. Succinite (Baltic amber)
2. Burmite (Burmese amber)
3. Simetite (Sicilian amber)
4. Rumanite (Rumanian amber).

The last three are considered to be the rarer forms.

The most abundant and prolific is Baltic amber, of which much is gathered along the shores of the Baltic Sea. Great storms battering the amber from the ocean floor finally throw it, together with flotsam, on to the beaches and among the rocks. Open-pit mining gives the greatest yield; here, giant steam shovels cut immense swathes from the "blue earth" in which landlocked amber is found.

Burmese amber is found in an area near to the Jadeite mines in the Hukong Valley. It is recovered only by mining. The principal colour of shards of this material varies from red to brown. In appearance, Burmite has a somewhat fluorescent look.

Sicilian amber is recovered from an area around the mouth of the Simeto River in Sicily. It generally displays the darker hues of red. Rumanian amber shows deeper colours of dark red, which may even be almost black in colour. This material often shows fluorescence.

In addition, amber is also found along the Samland Coast near Kalinigrad, Russia, as well as in the Dominican Republic, Czechoslovakia, Germany, Canada and the USA.

VITAL STATISTICS

Fossil amber originated as the life-giving saps of extinct coniferous trees, such as *Pinus Succinifera*, which flourished in the Eocene and Oligocene periods, just before the Ice Age, about 55 million years ago. It is found among sedimentary rocks.

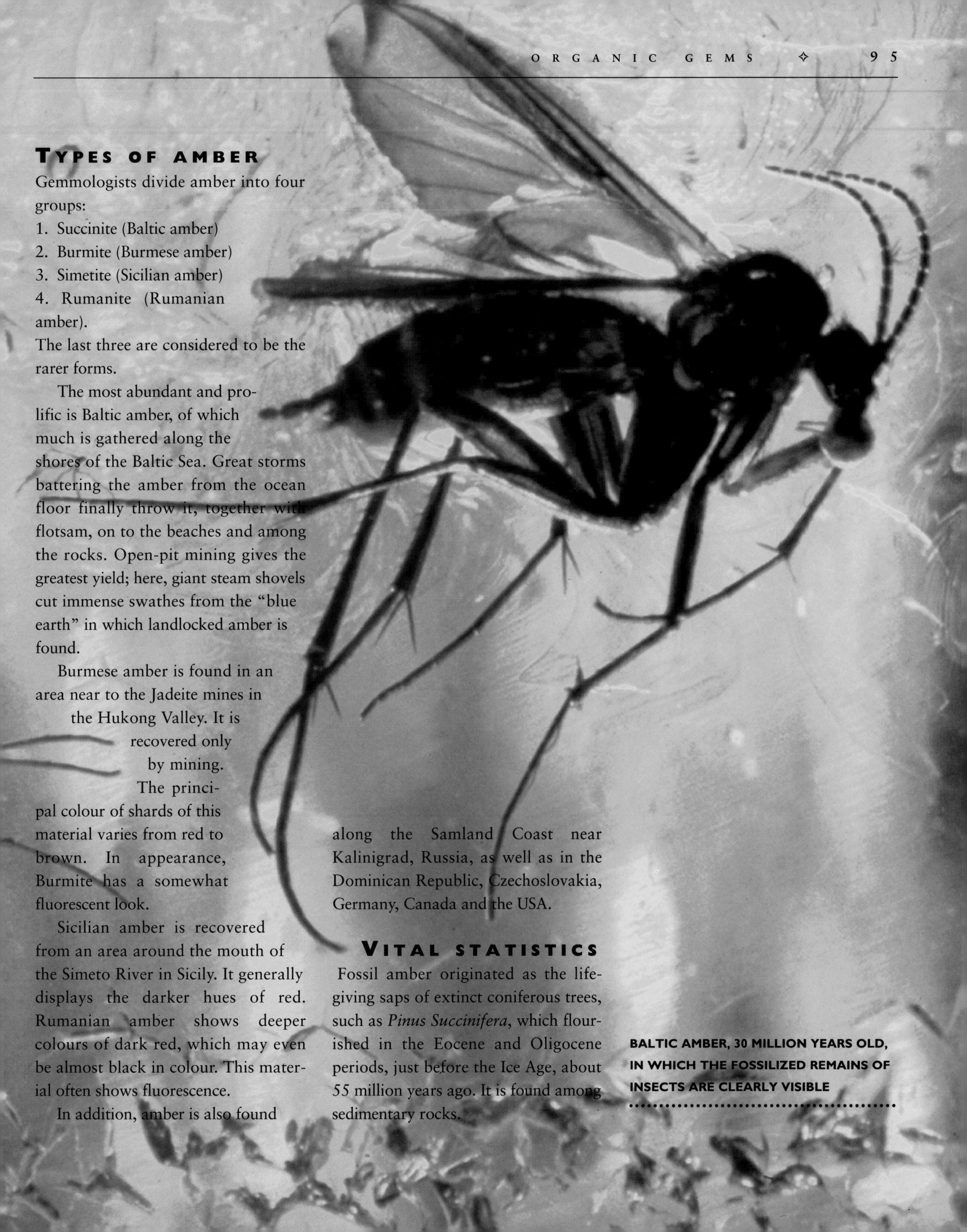

BALTIC AMBER, 30 MILLION YEARS OLD, IN WHICH THE FOSSILIZED REMAINS OF INSECTS ARE CLEARLY VISIBLE

FACT & FANTASY

IN DESCRIBING HIS WIFE'S HAIR COLOUR, NERO COMPARED IT TO AMBER. FROM THAT TIME ON, PLINY REPORTS THAT RESPECTABLE WOMEN "BEGAN TO ASPIRE TO THIS COLOUR."

MEDICINAL USES

For centuries, amber has been used medicinally in many ways, either as a cure or as a preventative measure. Pliny writes:

"Amber indeed is supposed to be a prophylactic against tonsillitis and other infections of the pharynx."

Listed by Dioscorides (AD 40–90) in his *Materia Medica*, together with some 200 other minerals and stones, amber is recommended as a useful healing agent by itself or an ingredient in medication.

TAKEN IN WINE

Callistratus advised that: "People subject to attacks of wild distraction" were usually cured when powdered amber was taken in a little wine. Immense confidence in the curative properties of amber was shown by the Romans – especially in the treatment of such ailments as fever, croup, asthma, hay fever and infections of the throat. To this end it was worn as a necklace or pendant.

For those who suffered painful ear problems, a medication of finely powdered amber, mixed with honey and rose oil, was put into the infected ear. Many Roman physicians, believing poor sight would be improved, recommended a mixture of amber powder and Attic honey to be taken internally. Only reddish ambers, however, were considered effective for medicinal purposes.

To quote Camillus Leonardus, physician to Cesare Borgia:

"Succinum or Amber being taken inwardly, it provokes urine, brings down the menses and facilitates a birth. It fastens teeth that are loosened..."

KEEPING THE FAITH

As the centuries passed, physicians retained their faith in amber. The seventeenth-century work, *A Lapidary or History of Pretious Stones*, 1652, states:

"The white odoriferous Amber is the best for physic use, and thought to be of great power and force against many diseases, as against vertigo and asthmaticall paroxysms, against catarrhes and arthreticall pains, against diseases of the stomach... and against diseases of the heart, against plagues, venoms and contagions. The Florentine Physicians are wont to prescribe some few drops of its oyl to be taken in wine for the former

THE *Legends* OF AMBER

purposes. It is used either in powder or in oyl..."

Another writer spoke of the power of amber "Lammer beads":

"Lammer beads... are almost always made of Amber, and are considered as a charm to keep away evil of every kind; their touch is believed to cure many diseases, and they are still worn by many old people in Scotland round the neck."

LOTIONS AND POTIONS

Prepared salts of amber were made by the medicine shops into all kinds of lotions, potions and electuaries. The virtue of such an amber preparation was said to be that it:

"heals, dryes, dissolves; strengthens heart and brain and revives the Animal and Vital Spirits by its sweet sulphur; and is used in perfumes to burn against bad air, and keep the Spirits from infection."

Time has not diminished our belief in amber as a

**AMBER PENDANTS
WERE THOUGHT TO CURE
ALL KINDS OF AILMENTS**

healer; it has retained its place as a medication in the armouries of both physician and pharmacist, in most countries. For example, a pungent oil distilled from amber is known as Oil of Succinate or Oil of Amber. This oily distillate has properties rather like turpentine and is used extensively in the preparation of liniments.

AMMONITE

"Hammonis Cornu [ammonite]... is among the most sacred stones of Ethiopia; [it] has a golden colour and is shaped like a ram's horn."

PLINY, IN *HISTORIA NATURALIS*

Ammonites cannot be regarded, in any sense whatsoever, as precious or semi-precious gemstones. They do, however, have an interesting history and attractive appearance, and are often seen on display at gemstone and mineral fairs.

Ammonites are the fossils of a long-extinct type of mollusc with a flat, spiral-shaped shell. Spiral fossil shells are found in profusion on land and in the sea. The shell is often filled in, or replaced completely, with a mineral such as pyrite or opal. Ammonites can reach about 30 cm in diameter. On display at Cardiff Museum, in Wales, is a massive ammonite fossil of about 2 m diameter, on which is carved the head of a snake.

THE RAM'S STONE
To the ancients, these fossils suggested the curved horns of the ram, and they were taken up by the people to symbolize their chosen deity. The story behind this runs as follows. Ammon of Thebes was one of the many deities worshipped in the temples of the Egyptian Middle Kingdom, around 1900 to 2000 BC. The cult of Ammon became very popular, and to make it more widely acceptable, the priests declared that he was another form of the god Ra, who was the chief deity, and named him Ammon-Ra.

Over the years, the principal symbol of Ammon was the ram with curved horns, and anything that suggested the shape of these horns came to be acknowledged as a symbol of Ammon-Ra. This symbol soon appeared as a talisman.

Pliny, in his *Historia Naturalis*, refers to the fossils as "Hammonis Cornu" which he says is "among the most sacred stones of Ethiopia; [it] has a golden yellow colour and is shaped like a ram's horn. The stone is guaranteed to ensure without fail dreams that will come true."

Camillus Leonardus adds to that and writes: "If a man puts himself in a posture of contemplation, the 'Hamonis' gives the mind a representation of all divine things."

ST HILDA'S STONES
During the centuries known as the Dark Ages, Europeans were dominated by

BELOW AND FAR RIGHT: A COLLECTION OF AMMONITES, FOSSIL MOLLUSCS FROM MANY MILLIONS OF YEARS AGO

THE *History* OF AMMONITES

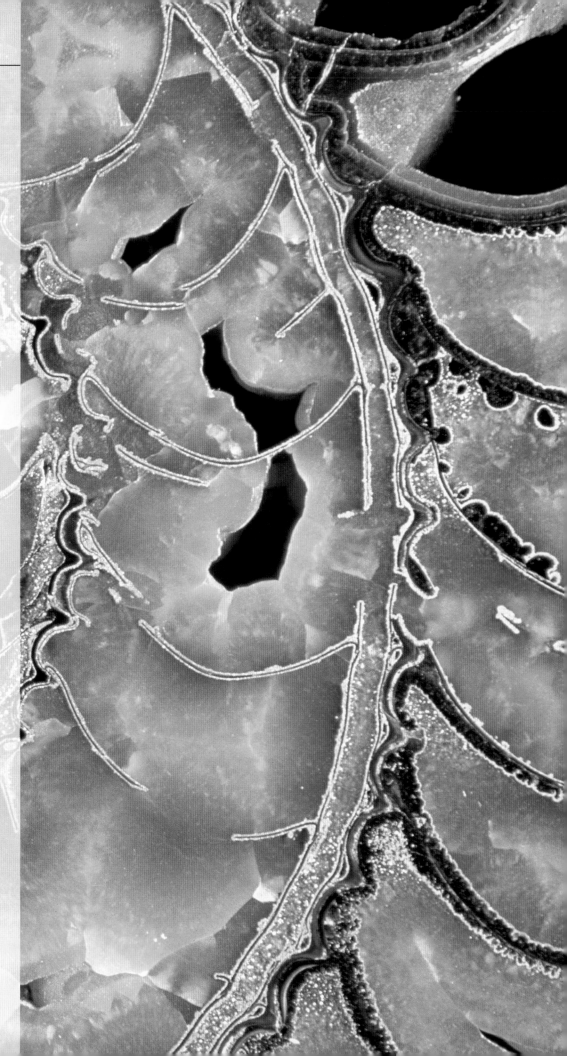

their beliefs in sorcery and witchcraft. With the spread of Christianity, pagan talismans and amulets were "taken over" by the bishops and given Christian symbolism.

One of those many talismans, ammonites, are associated with St Hilda – the first abbess of Whitby Abbey (AD 656), in the northeast of England.

Legend says that, when St Hilda came to Whitby to direct the affairs of the newly built abbey, the local people came and asked her for some very special help. They wanted her to intercede for them and pray to the Almighty to remove the snakes that infested the dale of the River Esk and the surrounding moors.

St Hilda promised to do this for them, and by means of contemplation and prayer the poisonous snakes began to coil up and roll over the cliffs, turning instantly to hard stone as they fell. Over the centuries, these ammonite fossils have therefore become known as St Hilda's stones, and have acquired a reputation for granting miraculous cures.

SYNTHETIC SNAKESTONES

Today, many ammonites are still found along the beaches and under the cliffs of northeast England.

Some years ago, the jet miners of Whitby (see page 110) found that they could make a little extra money by carving snakes' heads on the ammonites. They would then sell these stones to gullible visitors as authentic "St Hilda's snakestones".

CORAL

"In the pleased infant see its power expand when first the coral fills his little hand."

SPRAGUE, SOURCE UNKNOWN

C lose examination of coral reveals that it is made of an aggregate of coral polyp skeletons. These polyps are minute living creatures that live in vast colonies. When they die, their skeletal remains – mostly calcium carbonate – build up to form massive coral reefs.

The creatures themselves have a jellylike consistency when they are alive, and resemble tiny flowers. Viewed through a microscope lens, they look rather like daisies growing in a meadow.

It is genetic coding that determines how coral colonies build up and form their varied shapes and colourings. The most valuable variety from a gemmological point of view is the branch-like material named *Corallium Rubrum*, *Corralium Nobile* or, more commonly, "Precious coral". Types such as Brain Coral, Fan Coral and so on are mostly used as decorative pieces in the home.

CORAL FISHING

High-quality coral is chiefly fished from the warm waters of the western Mediterranean Sea around the coasts of Naples, Corsica, Catalonia and Provence. Fishermen in their small boats also dredge for coral along the coasts of Greece and the Greek islands, the Canary Islands, Tunisia, Morocco, Algeria, the Malaysian Archipelago, Japan, Northern Australia and in the Red Sea.

Coral is harvested with the aid of a wide, meshed net, held open by a sharp-edged iron frame. This simple device is dragged along the seabed among the coral reefs, where the frame snaps off coral branches and scoops them into the net.

BLACK AND BLUE

A black variety of coral (*Antipathes Spiralis*) is recovered from the sea off Hawaii, supplying a cottage industry that makes ornaments and jewellery sold in local shops and hotels. The Indian Ocean is another rich source of supply for the black variety. Unlike other corals, black coral is not a calcium carbonate. It is composed of an organic material known as chitin, which is related to human hair, human nails and the wool of sheep.

A blue variety (*Allopara Subirolcea*), fished around the Phillipines and the Cameroons, is usually made into beads that tend to resemble spheres of a

CORAL REEFS ARE MADE UP OF COUNTLESS TINY CREATURES

centre, while the innermost cells of the mantle manufacture calcium carbonate in the form of calcite flakes. These flakes are produced so that they overlap like tiles on a roof. This is the layer that forms the smooth and beautiful Mother of Pearl bed on which the soft animal rests; the pearly lining seen inside many mollusc shells.

EASING IRRITATION

When a "foreign body" gets inside the mollusc shell, such as a piece of grit, or a worm that has bored through the shell, the mollusc tries to ease the irritation that this causes by forming a layer of "nacre" (calcium carbonate) over the intrusion and cementing it to its shell. This bulge on the shell, called a blister pearl, may eventually be removed and used as a jewel.

Spherical pearls are formed when a foreign body makes a depression in the mantle in such a way that a sac eventually develops around the irritant, which then becomes entombed in nacre. The size of the pearl depends on the amount of nacre laid over the irritant. Eventually, the pearl itself becomes the foreign body, and starts to be overlaid with more nacre.

CARING FOR PEARLS

Because pearls contain around 2 per cent water, keeping them in a warm place, such as near a radiator, may cause them to dry out and develop hairline cracks and fissures. And they will almost certainly lose their lustre. Wear them frequently, and always keep them clean. Strings of pearls can be cleaned by "stirring" them lightly in potato flour, which removes perspiration and many other surface blemishes.

FACT & FANTASY

LARGE, BEAUTIFUL PINK PEARLS, PATTERNED ON THEIR SURFACE WITH ATTRACTIVE FLAME MARKINGS, ARE A PRODUCT OF THE GREAT CONCH MOLLUSC, WHOSE HOME IS THE WARM WATERS OF THE GULF OF CALIFORNIA.

PEARLS CULTURED FROM FRESHWATER MUSSELS

CULTURED PEARL

Genuine pearls are comparatively rare and expensive, and so a means was invented whereby molluscs could be induced to mass-produce them.

CHINESE CULTIVATION

The art of pearl cultivation may well have been first practised by the Chinese, during the thirteenth century. Crude pearls were made by inserting an irritant, such as a piece of grit, between the mantle and the shell, causing the mollusc to cover the foreign body with nacre.

A particular speciality of the very early pearl makers was the insertion of small waxen images of Buddha into the oyster, which would duly become coated with nacre. When they had become sufficiently coated, the images were removed and the attractive pearly figures were sold in the temples, in aid of charity.

STEP BY STEP

The process of pearl cultivation is very simple and the mollusc used is usually a type of oyster. A spherical bead of Mother of Pearl, along with a small piece of mantle taken from a donor oyster, is inserted into the mantle of the receiving oyster. The prepared oysters, several hundred at a time, are placed in wire cages, and hundreds of these cages are suspended in the sea beneath a special type of raft.

The oysters are harvested after three to four years – the epithelial cells of the inserted mantle by then having performed their task of inducing the coating of the bead with nacre. The thickness of nacre is determined by the length of time a bead has spent in the mollusc. Two to three years is roughly the time it takes for the oyster to deposit about ½ mm of nacre on a 5 mm diameter bead.

Of the hundreds of thousands of prepared oysters suspended in the cages, around 50 per cent die. This may be as a result of natural causes, attacks by starfish or from being smothered by a certain type of red plankton. When this plankton invades an area of water, it appears to turn the sea red – a phenomenon known as "The Red Tide".

The oysters left in the baskets produce the following: around 10 per cent poor quality pearl, 20 per cent saleable pearl, 15 per cent good quality pearl and 5 per cent excellent pearl. The poorest quality pearls are sent for crushing and processing into the fine calcium carbonate powders used in some cosmetics and medicines.

CULTURED HUES

The small *Pinctada* oyster is commonly used to produce cultured pearls. There are several varieties, three of which are named after the colour of the edge of the mantle, namely: Silver Lip, Gold Lip and Black Lip. The first produces white nacre, the second pink to yellowish and the black lip usually provides blackish pearls.

Industries providing black pearls gathered from Black Lip oysters have expanded in towns and villages along the coasts of the Gulf of Mexico and certain islands of the South Seas – the nature of the water in those areas is thought to provide a particular type of nutrient.

CULTURED PEARLS HAVE THE SAME SOFT SHEEN AS THE "REAL THING"

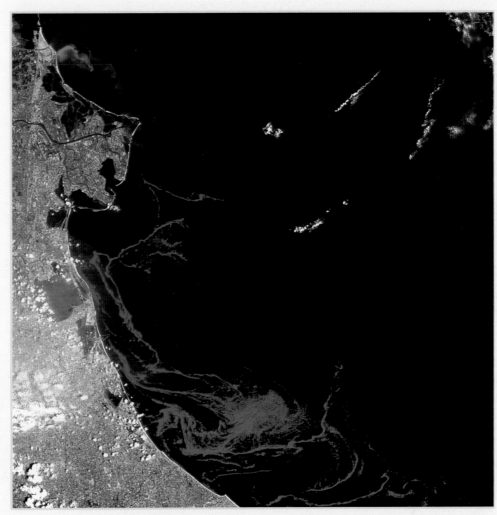

ALGAE SEEN FROM SPACE. FEEDING ON RIVER SILT, IT STOPS PEARL GROWTH.

••

Oysters may, on occasion, become disturbed. When this happens, a layer of conchiolin (which makes up the outer shell) is deposited over the nacre of the pearl forming at that time. After the disturbance has abated, the oyster produces nacre once again, but the conchiolin layer shows through and colours the pearl brown, black, blue or grey.

Of course, people have not been slow to ply their trade in the alteration of pearl colour. Cultured pearls of an intense black colour have probably been treated with silver nitrate, which will inhibit fluorescence generated by blue light when viewed through a red filter; natural black pearls show this fluorescence as a dim red glow.

PEARL LOOK-ALIKES

No synthetic material came anywhere near the lustre of nacre until paints were developed that contained fish scales. This is applied to the insides of hollow glass beads, which are then filled with wax. Alternatively, paint can be applied to the surface of strong, hollow glass beads, which are then placed in a drying kiln before being highly burnished.

PEARLS HAVE BEEN LINKED TO THE BEAUTIFUL GODDESS DIANA, DEITY OF THE GREEN FORESTS AND OF YOUNG WOMEN

As an emblem of purity, innocence and peace, the pearl was once thought to be sacred to the Moon and to the goddess Diana. It was for these reasons that, in ancient times, young virgin girls wore the emblem of Diana – and so invoked her protection.

DEW-DROPS

Legends surrounding the origin of pearls have no doubt added to their desirability. At one time there existed a belief, well recorded by Pliny in his *Historia Naturalis*, that pearls were the end product of dew. He wrote that pearls are the product of dew falling into open oyster shells at breeding time:

"The quality," he continued, "varies with the amount of dew received; being lustrous if the dew was pure and dull if foul. Cloud spoilt the colour, lightning

stopped the growth, but thunder made the shellfish miscarry and eject hollow husks called physemata (bubbles). Rainbows always being used to the best advantage."

Arabian writers of antiquity have added to this myth by recording that, on the 16th of Nisan, or April, pearl oysters "rise from the seabed and open their shells to receive the rain which falls at that time; the drops thus gathered become pearls."

DEAD MAN'S FINGER

The origins of a macabre ritual practised by the pearl fishers of Borneo have been lost in the corridors of time. Every ninth pearl recovered during a dive was reverently set aside for the ceremony of "the breeding of the pearls", which was performed to ensure a good pearl harvest.

On the return of the fishing fleet to shore, all the saved ninth pearls were placed in a bottle, together with two grains of rice for each pearl. The bottle was stoppered with the finger of a dead man and, with solemn ceremony, hung in the branches of a tree. Grave robbers supplied the necessary fingers for the ceremony. However, in recent times, the administrators of the island have outlawed that particular gruesome practice, and modern pearl fishers use a more acceptable stopper.

DRAGONS, ELEPHANTS, AND LOVE POTIONS

Chinese mystics say that dragons are rainmakers, and that, when they spit, some of their spittle is of pearls. And so, they conclude, rain and pearls fall when dragons are fighting in the heavens. For its association with rain, many Chinese people consider pearl to be an effective talisman against fire.

Hindu folklore notes that, on occasion, pearls are found in the stomach, forehead or brain of an elephant. These are avidly sought as powerful talismans against all kinds of danger. Hindu astrological terms present a pearl as

THE Legends ◆ OF PEARL

associated with the moon and consider that pearls are representative of lovers. This is why a major constituent of traditional Hindu love potions is finely powdered pearl.

A similar belief in pearl as the lover's gem, and in the power of similar potions, became a feature of life in most of Europe during the seventeenth century. Unfortunately, those who bought twists of powdered pearl from medicine shops at that time were usually cheated; genuine pearls were far beyond the means of ordinary people.

A CURE FOR ALL MALADIES

All kinds of other uses were found for pearls. Thirteenth-century physicians treated ailments of the heart with medicines containing powdered pearl and such medicines were thought effective against poisoning in the 1500s. Powdered pearl suspended in distilled water was even administered to Charles V1 of France in an unsuccessful attempt to restore his sanity.

Drs Johannes Schroeder and William Rowland claimed that pearl medicines

CHINESE FOLKLORE STATES THAT, WHEN DRAGONS ARE FIGHTING IN THE HEAVENS, PEARLS RAIN DOWN ON THE EARTH BELOW

FACT & FANTASY

FINELY GROUND POWDER OF PEARL, SIMILAR IN TEXTURE TO FLOUR, BEGAN TO BE USED COSMETICALLY BY THE LADIES OF FRANCE, REPLACING DANGEROUS COSMETIC POWDERS (SOME INCLUDED ARSENIC) SUPPLIED BY LOCAL MEDICINE SHOPS. THIS WAS BELIEVED TO GREATLY "IMPROVE THE TEXTURE AND LUSTRE OF THE SKIN".

were so potent that "men in the greatest agonies are refreshed thereby." S. M. Tagore believed that: "it cures the vomiting of blood; relieves haemorrhoids, strictures of the bowel and excessive menstruation; cures jaundice, all diseases of the heart, and removes evil spirits from the minds of men." Rubbed over the body with other medicines, he informs us that leprosy is also cured, but adds that, to avoid damaging the patient's brain, the pearl must be burned together with coral.

Modern medicine, too, has a use for pearls – both natural and cultured. These are the pearls rejected as gems by the pearl fisheries and farms. They are processed and ground to a very fine powder and provide the pharmaceutical industry with a valuable source of calcium. And the cosmetic industry adds pearls to face powders and creams.

JET

"Your lustre too'll draw courtship to you as iet [jet] doth straw."

BEN JOHNSON, PLAYWRIGHT (1572–1637)

Jet started life as rotten wood. Over millions of years it has been buried and compressed into a type of coal. From this humble material, all kinds of beautiful objects have been fashioned.

LONGSTANDING REPUTATION

Over the centuries, jet gained an international reputation as an ornamental material that took and retained a high polish particularly well. In addition to this, it was easily worked and could be skilfully shaped and carved into all kinds of desirable body ornaments, both large and small.

The material itself has a waxy lustre and at times contains small pyrite inclusions. Briskly rubbing jet with a cloth causes this fossil material to become charged with static electricity, and while in this state it has the ability to attract small pieces of tissue or straw.

MAGICAL PROPERTIES

Large deposits of jet have been known to exist in the Whitby area of northeast England since the Bronze Age. The Romans, who mined jet extensively during their occupation of England, attributed magical properties to it. The Vikings, too, exploited English jet deposits, and so it is not altogether surprising that numerous Whitby jet artifacts have been unearthed and recovered in Iceland.

An awareness of the magical properties of jet were also handed on to successive generations of magi, and the

Venerable Bede (eighth century) writes: "In the burning, the perfume thereof chaseth away serpents... The magicians use this jet stone much in their sorceries with red hot axes, for they affirm that the jet being cast thereupon will burn and consume, and that which you wish and desire shall happen accordingly."

Pliny tells us that jet is ignited by water. What he really meant, but didn't understand, is that spontaneous combustion of most coal material is aided by the presence of moisture. "The kindling of jet," he says, "drives off snakes and relieves suffocation of the uterus. Its fumes detect

THE *History* ◆ OF JET

attempts to simulate a disabling illness or confirm a state of virginity."

He writes also that, when jet is boiled in wine, the resultant elixir cures toothache; if combined with a soft wax and spread over them, scrofulous tumours are healed.

COTTAGE INDUSTRY

The northeast of England has been famous for its deposits of jet since St Hilda became the first abbess of Whitby Abbey in the 600s (see also pages 98–99). Deposits of jet uncovered in the vicinity of the abbey provided material for a lucrative cottage industry run by the nuns. The abbey workshops made crucifixes and strung rosaries for their own use, and surplus production was sold to the many pilgrims and visitors who came there.

Cardano, writing in the sixteenth century, refers to jet as "Black Amber", from which beads were made into intricate rosaries. He also mentions curiously carved jet figurines imported from Spain into Italy. Powdered jet, added to water or wine, was believed to have had medicinal powers.

MOURNING JEWELLERY

Jewellery has always been worn in remembrance of the dead, but it was not until the British monarch Queen Victoria retired into mourning on the death of Prince Albert, in 1861, that mourning jewellery carved from jet became fashionable.

THE Legends
◆ OF JET

SAINT HILDA 614-680 AD, FIRST ABBESS OF WHITBY, COUNSELS A VISITOR

Soon, every family in the land possessed some artefact fashioned from jet. Whitby, as the leading producer of quality jet, became the centre of excellence for carved jewellery. The highly skilled Whitby craftsmen fashioned carved beads, polished beads for rosaries, bracelets and earrings, hair ornaments and cameo rings. And, because jet is such a light material, they carved it into enormous, intricate brooches.

Great quantities of cannel coal were made into mourning jewellery, but these artefacts were never quite as black as jet. Cannel coal is easily distinguished from jet as it has a slight brownish tinge when the two are compared.

FACT & FANTASY

A COMMON SUBSTITUTE FOR JET IS ANOTHER FOSSIL FUEL KNOWN AS CANNEL COAL. THIS IS SIMILAR IN CONSTRUCTION TO JET BUT IS OF A SOMEWHAT INFERIOR QUALITY. THE NAME CANNEL MEANS CANDLE AND REFERS TO THE WAXES EXTRACTED FROM THIS TYPE OF COAL, WHICH WERE ONCE SUPPLIED TO MANUFACTURERS OF WAX CANDLES.

3 *Mythical* STONES

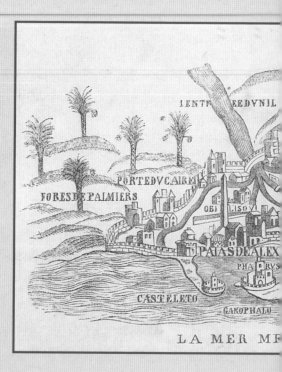

The power of gemstones is such that, as well as the better-known organic and inorganic stones around us, other stones have crept into popular folklore. Some of these are entirely mythical in origin, it seems, while others are real enough, but are surrounded by a magical aura. A selection of these follows.

ABRAXAS

"Many people who are terrified of the plague... try to ward it off by the use of certain words and figures, particularly the word 'abracadabra' formed into a triangle."

DANIEL DEFOE, WRITER (1660-1731)

The North African city of Alexandria started as a village of tents, sitting astride the crossroads of the world's trade routes, and grew into what was once the main commercial and cultural centre of the Middle East. Traders brought their wares to this glittering city from countries as widespread as Persia, India, Asia Minor and the many lands occupied by the Romans. Most importantly, they also brought their own very special beliefs, practices and religions.

FACT & FANTASY

THE CODES OF "NUMEROLOGY" ALSO APPEARED ON VARIOUS TALISMAN STONES. NUMEROLOGY CAN BE DESCRIBED AS A BELIEF IN THE POWERS THOUGHT TO RESIDE IN MAGICAL WORDS OR COMBINATIONS OF WORDS. IT WAS SKILFULLY USED BY GNOSTIC PRIESTS AND EARLY CHRISTIANS ALIKE. THE SYSTEM RAN AS FOLLOWS. COUPLED WITH EACH LETTER OF THE GREEK ALPHABET WAS A NUMBER. THE NUMBERS THEMSELVES HAD NO SIGNIFICANCE, BUT THE FINAL FIGURE OBTAINED BY THE ADDITION OF ALL THE NUMBERS ASSIGNED TO A CERTAIN COMBINATION OF LETTERS – SAY, A NAME – INDICATED ITS HIDDEN POWER. SOMETIMES, THESE GREEK LETTERS WERE COMBINED WITH ASTROLOGICAL FORMULAS AND ENGRAVED ON ONE OF THE MANY CHALCEDONIES IN AN ATTEMPT TO ATTRACT GOOD INFLUENCES.

THE GNOSTICS

Among the people living in Alexandria's teeming streets was a religious sect whose followers called themselves Gnostics – "those who know". They claimed to possess a knowledge (gnosis) denied to lesser mortals, which appeared to be a particular conception of the conflict between good and evil. They also adopted many of the philosophical ideologies, rites and talismans used in older religions. Alarmed by the rapid growth in numbers of gnostics, the prevailing Coptic Church eventually came to regard them as excommunicable heretics.

Many gnostics held the belief that their god, Abraxas, was the only supreme being. He was depicted as having the torso and arms of a human and the head of a cockerel, representing the virtue of foresight. The body is supported on legs formed of serpents, which represent the mind and "the word". On one arm he supports the shield of wisdom; in his

ALEXANDRIA, OFTEN SEEN AS THE FIRST GREAT COSMOPOLITAN CITY
•••••••••••••••••••••••••••••••••••••••

other hand he grasps the whip of power.

This figure of Abraxas appeared on all kinds of amulets and talismans, mostly fashioned from chalcedonies such as carnelian, agate, bloodstone, jasper and onyx. Included in the many professional duties of gnostic priests was the preparation of suitable designs for engraving on compatible stones to form precious talismans.

ABRACADABRA

Some of these stone talismans had words said to have magical properties engraved on them. One particular word spell, borrowed from the ancient Sumer-Babylonian civilizations, is in the form of a diminishing pattern. The spell is in use even today, particularly in Central Europe. The origins of this word spell lie in an ancient Chaldean phrase, "*abrada ke dabra*" – meaning, to "perish like the word" – which became corrupted to

"abracadabra". In creating this talisman it was necessary for the word to be repeated successively beneath itself, with one letter omitted on each line, until the last line was simply as engraved "A".

ABRACADABRA
BRACADABRA
RACADABRA
ACADABRA
CADABRA
ADABRA
DABRA
ABRA
BRA
RA
A

This abracadabra charm was much used in England during the Great Plague of 1665 by Arabian physicians who had come to help care for the victims.

THE DECLINE

The second century saw the beginning of the end of gnosticism. This was its inevitable destiny when the Roman Empire, adopting Christianity, started to stamp out competing religions. However, the new religion did not, or possibly could not, forbid the making and using of amulets or talismans and the banished gnostic priests continued to dispense them. In the centuries since then, all kinds of beautifully engraved Abraxas stones have been found in Middle Eastern countries once occupied by the Romans.

•••••••••••••••••••••••••••••••••••••••
ABRAXAS STONES WERE SAID TO DRIVE AWAY DEMONS AND DEVILS

BEZOAR

"Everything that frees the body from any ailment is called the Bezoar of that ailment."

CAMILLUS LEONARDUS,
16TH-CENTURY PHYSICIAN

B ezoar is the name given by some peoples through history to stones recovered from the stomachs of certain animals – especially stags and goats that are indigenous to a block of land from the Middle East to China.

These stones are usually composed mainly of phosphate of lime, but may also be principally phosphate of ammonia or magnesia. They are believed to exert all kinds of healing powers, especially dispelling poison and curing poisonous diseases. Today, this belief is still held in the area around Iran.

ORIGINS

The Middle Eastern name for this highly coveted and remarkable stone is *pad-zahr*, or "poison expelling" – *pad*: "to dislodge" and *zahr*: "poison". European tongues, however, found these difficult to say and pronounced the two words as bezoar.

The earliest peoples who knew of the stone and wrote about its powers were the Persians (now Iran) and the Arabs. One important Persian medical work, compiled by Mohammed ben Mansur sometime during the twelfth century,

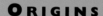
THIS ILLUSTRATION, SHOWING BEZOAR BEING EXTRACTED FROM THE HEAD OF A TOAD COMES FROM THE 1483 EDITION OF HORTUS *SANITATIS*, ONE OF THE EARLIEST MEDICAL TEXTS

states that the stone was greatly prized for use as a talisman when it was carved as a small image of the Shah.

Knife handles often included intricately carved bezoar – as the handle came into contact with the user's skin, it was thought to guard against the possibility of poisoning. Scrapings of the stone were also added to food or drink.

THE GREAT PLAGUE

Bezoar does not appear to have been known in Europe until recommended by Arab physicians in the fight against the Great Plague. In parts of India and China, where the stone is known as *Mo-So*, the bezoar is credited with an ability to bestow renewed youth and beauty.

FACT & FANTASY

THE VIRTUES OF BEZOAR WERE TAKEN SERIOUSLY BY ROYALTY AND THE NOBILITY. AN ENTRY IN THE INVENTORY OF EMPEROR CHARLES V'S JEWELS MENTIONS:
"... A BOX OF BLACK LEATHER LINED WITH CRIMSON VELVET, CONTAINING FOUR BEZOAR STONE, VARIOUSLY SET IN GOLD." THE EMPEROR DIRECTED THAT ONE OF THESE STONES WAS TO BE GIVEN TO WILLIAM VAN MALE, HIS "GENTLEMAN OF THE CHAMBER, BEING SICK, AS IT WAS SUSPECTED, OF THE PLAGUE."

The many virtues attributed to the stone by the Persians are just as highly valued by the peoples of Malaysia. Here, red coloured monkeys of the species *Semnopithicus* develop a bezoar known as the Guliga. A rarer and more highly prized stone – the Guliga Landak – is recovered from the feral porcupine, whose habitat is the Malaysian forests. Many of these stones are exported to Afghanistan where, among its other well known attributes, bezoar is used as a remedy for asthma.

It has also been prescribed by Eastern physicians as a remedy for diseases of the kidneys and bladder. Treatment at one time consisted mainly of tying the stone as near as possible to the affected organ.

In Iran today, bezoars gathered for medical use are taken from the stomachs of the wild goat (*Caprea Acyagros*). The demand for these stones is apparently unlimited and the larger bezoars generally command a price equal to their weight in gold.

According to Joseph de Acosta (*Histoire Naturelle et Morales des Indes*, 1600), the peoples of Peru had formed their own theory about the origin of the Bezoar. He writes:

"The Indians relate from the teachings of their ancestors that in the province of Xaura, and other provinces in Peru, there are various poisonous herbs and animals which poison the waters where the Vicunas drink and eat.

Of these poisonous herbs, one is right well known by natural instinct to the vicuna and to other animals which engender the bezoar, and they eat of this herb and thus preserve themselves from the poison of the waters and the pastures."

"The Indians also say that the stone is formed in the stomachs of these animals from this herb, whence comes the virtue it possesses as an antidote for poisons, as well as its other marvellous properties."

An early traveller called Garnet recorded the origin of a particular type of bezoar, as described to him by Arab peoples:

"When the Hart is sick and has eaten many serpents for his recovery, he is brought to so great a heat that he hasten to the water and there covereth his body unto the very ears and eyes at which distilleth many tears from which the stone is engendered."

SNAKE STONE

"Among other stones there is one in the possession of a conjuror remarkable for its brilliance and beauty, but more so for the extraordinary manner in which it is found..."

TIMBERLAKE, SEVENTEENTH-CENTURY WRITER

One of the few writings to give a superficial description of snake stones is the fourth-century Greek poem *Lithica*. In this poem they are described as black, round, rough, hard and weighty spheres, furrowed with many wavy lines. They are said to be recovered from the heads of snakes. The magi used these weighty stones as talismans in their war against the malignant forces of evil.

SNAKE CHARMERS

The Sampoori – Indian snake charmers – claim to be skilled in the art of extracting these stones from the heads of snakes. In *Discourse of the Travels of Two English Pilgrims* (Timberlake, 1611), there is a description of a fabulous jewel supposedly taken from the head of a giant snake and used in conjuring. It reads:

"It grew, if we may credit the Indians, in the head of a monstrous serpent, whose retreat was by its brilliancy discovered. But a great number of snakes attending him, he being, I suppose by his diadem, of superior rank among the serpents, made it dangerous to attack him... Many were the attempts by the Indians, but all were frustrated, till a fellow more bold than the rest, casing himself in leather impenetrable to the bite of the serpent, or his guards, and watching a convenient opportunity, surprised and killed him, tearing the jewel from its head.

"This stone the conjuror had kept hid for many years in some place unknown to all but two women who have steadfastly refused large presents to destroy it lest some signal judgement or mischance should follow... That such a stone exists, I believe, having seen many of great beauty, but I cannot think it could answer all the ecomiums the Indians bestow upon it. The conjuror, I suppose, hatched the account of its discovery."

ANTIDOTE TO SNAKE VENOM

To be effective as an antidote to snake venom, a snake-stone must be applied to the bite before the venom has time to invade the nervous system. Apparently the stone is seen to cling to the bite for a short time and, when its work is completed and it has absorbed all the poison, it drops off. For successful use, two stones were required, each replacing the other as they became saturated with snake venom.

LIKENESS TO TABASHEER

G. F. Kunz, the eminent gemmologist, writes that he had examined a number of snake or serpent stones sent to him from India. He believes, like many others, that these stones were more than likely to have been tabasheer (see pages 118–119).

COBRA STONES

Called by the Portuguese *cobras de capello*, these stones were reputedly taken from the heads of snakes that had a hood – that is, Cobras, or *Serpens pilosus* – for it was under the hood that the stone was said to be found.

Tavernier has recorded in his writings that soaking the stones in milk freed them from the poison; they were rendered fit for re-use when the milk became thickened and greenish yellow in colour. A freely translated paragraph taken from his *Travels* reads:

"This stone being rubbed against another stone, yields a certain slime, which being drank in water by that person that has the poison in his body, powerfully drives it out. The serpents are nowhere to be found but upon the coasts of Melinde; but for the stones, you may buy them of the Portugueze mariners and soldiers that come from Mozambique."

PASSING THE TEST

Tavernier goes on to describe two methods of testing the stones: "The first is to place one in the mouth; it should cleave to the palate. The second test is to place one in a tumbler of water which should begin to seethe, and small bubbles will rise from the stone to the surface."

Albertus Magnus (1193–1280), one-time Bishop of Ratisbon, is reported to have carried a stone that guarded against epidemics, evil magic and the bites of serpents.

According to a report carried in the medical journal, the *Lancet*, a Boer farmer owned a serpent stone that he loaned to neighbours in their time of need. When the daughter of an English hunter was bitten by a snake, the father sent a messenger to borrow the stone. Because of a delay, the stone wasn't applied to the bite until several hours later, and this was said to have prevented the wound from healing properly.

TABASHEER

"... the charm and virtue of the stones were such that those who wore them would never perish by steel."

MARCO POLO (1254–1324)

A particular species of bamboo growing in Malaysia and Indonesia is known by the peoples of those countries as *bulu kasap* or *mambu* – both effectively meaning "rough bamboo". The cane exudes a substance called *sacar mambus*, or "sugar of mambu", which collects in the joints of the cane. It forms as a sticky fluid that is further thickened by evaporation until a bluish white solid remains. The solid has the appearance of a thick splinter of sea shell and this is known in the West as tabasheer.

This "stone" was known and used in medicine by Aviccena, Grand Vizier and Surgeon to the Sultan of Turkey in the tenth century. It has also been used by Malaysian and Indonesian physicians and pharmacists, ground to a very fine powder. This powder is known to the general public as *mali mali rotan jer'-nauf* – "blood of the dragon Rattan" and by the medical profession simply as "bamboo salt".

FIGHTING STONE

An eighteenth-century Dutch writer tells us of the highly valued Malaysian "mestica stone", a stone that was found in a plant and gave fighting men immunity from harm. This invulnerability was conferred upon any warrior who carried several of the stones into battle. These stones were so tightly bound to the skin that they eventually became embedded in the flesh. Several Dutch army officers on leave from Malaysia confirmed meeting with such men.

FACT & FANTASY

IN MALAYSIA AND INDONESIA, IT IS SAID THAT A TALISMAN OF TABASHEER SET IN GOLD WILL REMOVE PAST, PRESENT AND FUTURE ANXIETIES.

TABASHEER IS THE NAME GIVEN TO THE HARDENED STICKY SUBSTANCE THAT COLLECTS IN THE JOINTS OF A CERTAIN KIND OF BAMBOO

MARCO POLO

Not much is known in Europe about tabasheer, but it is highly prized in the East. Marco Polo's account of an expedition mounted by the Great Kahn against the Island of Chipangu (Japan) states:

"When the people of the Kahn had landed on the Great Island they stormed a tower belonging to some islanders who refused to surrender. Any resistance being overcome, the Kahn's soldiers cut off the heads of all the garrison except eight. On these eight they found it impossible to inflict any wound. Now this was by virtue of certain stones which they had in their arms inserted between the skin and flesh with such skill as not to show externally."

He goes on:

"And the charm and virtue of the stones were such that those who wore them would never perish by steel. So when the Kahn's generals heard this they ordered that the prisoners be beaten to death with wooden clubs. After their death the stones were extracted from their bodies and were highly prized."

HEALING TABASHEER

Until comparatively recently, tabasheer had been used extensively in Malaysia and Indonesia as a powerful ingredient in medications for the treatment of eye problems. The Crusaders, too, learned of the healing properties of Oriental tabasheer and used it in their hospital on Rhodes for the treatment of fevers, stomach complaints and infections of the liver.

The kind of melancholia that manifests itself during long periods of isolation was also reported to respond well to treatment in which tabasheer was the prime ingredient. As already mentioned on pages 116 to 117, tabasheer may actually be the mysterious "snake stones" used by various peoples as an antidote to venomous bites.

ABOVE: MARCO POLO CAME ACROSS MAGICAL STONES ON HIS TRAVELS

THE *Legends* ◆ OF TABASHEER

TOAD STONE

"Sweet are the uses of adversity;
Which, like the toad, ugly and venomous,
Wears yet a precious jewel in his head."

SHAKESPEARE (FROM *AS YOU LIKE IT*)

Those claiming to have seen toad stones say that they are like white, brown or blackish pebbles and are found in the head of a toad. This creature was believed to have such a great fear of man that he spat poison at him. Therefore, the stone in its head came to be considered an antidote to any form of poison.

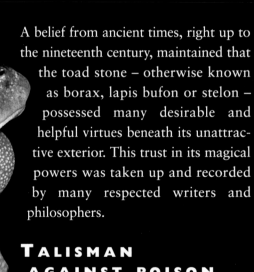

A belief from ancient times, right up to the nineteenth century, maintained that the toad stone – otherwise known as borax, lapis bufon or stelon – possessed many desirable and helpful virtues beneath its unattractive exterior. This trust in its magical powers was taken up and recorded by many respected writers and philosophers.

TALISMAN AGAINST POISON

This was another stone valued by people of high rank who were fearful of being poisoned by rivals for power. Along with

DUTCH THEOLOGIAN AND HUMANIST ERASMUS DICTATES TO HIS SCRIBE
···

bezoar, snake stones, tabasheer and so many others, this was seen as an important antidote to venom, and high prices were paid for it.

The stone was prescribed to be worn set in a gold ring, in such a manner that the stone touched the finger. If poison was near, it was said, the stone became very hot and gave its warning by burning the finger.

THE PROVING OF THE STONE

The provenance of toad stone is described by Lupton in his *Book of Notable Things*. He writes:

THE *Legends*
◆ OF TOAD STONE

ERASMVS.

"You shall know whether the tode stone be the ryghte or perfect stone or not. Hold the stone before a tode so that he may see it, and if it be a ryghte and true stone, the tode will leape towarde it, and make as though to snatch it. He envieth so much that none should have the stone." Toad stones were reported to be in great demand by witches and

---

FACT & FANTASY

A TOAD STONE ANTIDOTE PRESCRIBED BY MANY EMINENT PHYSICIANS CONSISTED QUITE SIMPLY OF A SMALL AMOUNT OF SCRAPINGS COLLECTED FROM THE STONE, WHICH WERE TO BE TAKEN IN WINE OR WATER.

---

hags as the activating ingredient in magical brews.

The learned scholar Erasmus (1465–1536) describes a certain stone:

"set at the feet of our Lady Walsingham to which no name has been given by the Greeks and Romans, but the French have named it after the toad in as much as it represents the figure so exactly that no art of man could do it as well... And the wonder is so much the greater that the stone is very small. The figure of the toad does not project from the surface, but shines through, as if enclosed in the stone itself. And some – no mean authorities – add that if the stone be put in vinegar the toad will swim therein and move its legs."

A SCOTTISH CHARM

Lhuyd, the Curator of the Ashmolean Museum, mentions in a lecture given in 1699 that Scottish Highlanders placed great faith in the power of the toad stone to protect and prevent their houses from burning and their boats from sinking. No commander would enter battle without one, for he believed that to do so would surely bring defeat.

FAIRY MAGIC

A belief that fairies stole children away was once part of a widespread folklore. Shakespeare's *Midsummer Night's Dream* gives witness to this when Oberon and Titania quarrel over a changeling boy.

To prevent this, amulets of toadstone set in gold were bought by those who could afford them, and worn as pendants by their children. A letter written during the 1880s describes such an amulet as protecting a child "from the power of the fairies".

THE GREAT SCHOLAR ERASMUS WROTE ABOUT A MAGICAL TOAD STONE

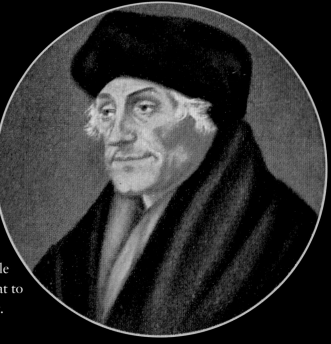

SOME OTHER MYTHICAL STONES

LAPIS ALECTORIUS

Both Pliny and Camillus Leonardus were acquainted with alectorius; it was known as a stone of magic rather than a thing of beauty. Both writers give fairly similar descriptions. Lapis Alectorius was seen as a bright, transparent and crystal-like stone, occasionally marked with pinkish veins. Most ancient writers say the stone was generated in the gizzard of a capon and was about the size of a bean.

To ensure the effectiveness of this magical stone, strict instructions for its development were laid down by the magi. Firstly, the bird in question must have been castrated on reaching its third year of life. Secondly, the stone was not to be harvested until the capon had reached at least its seventh year. When the bird refused to drink as he ate, then alectorius was judged to be ready for removal.

SKILLS AND STRENGTH

Milo of Croton (6 BC) – the great wrestler and strong man of his time – constantly carried an alectorius with him. He claimed that he owed his strength and skill to the influence of the stone, and only from the time of its loss did his talents desert him.

The Romans credited alectorius with the power to cast a cloak of invisibility over its owner, while, at some time during the Middle Ages, a belief became established that he who owned alectorius would never go thirsty.

DOMESTIC PEACE

It was also claimed that the stone brought domestic peace and harmony and that, when it was worn either as a pendant or as a ring by a wife who had erred, she regained favour in her husband's eyes.

Alectorius was reputed to confer the gift of persuasion, victory and honour on its fortunate owner. It also conferred the gift of eloquence when slipped under the tongue.

LAPIS DRACONIUS

Draconius is taken – so we are told – from the heads of dragons or great snakes dwelling in dark caverns, deep within the mountainous countries of the Far East. Some said that it was black in colour and pyramidal in form; others that it was colourless and transparent and could not be worked in any way.

"The draconius," says Albertus Magnus (1193–1280), sometime bishop of Ratisbon, "must be removed from the heads of the dragons while they lay panting, for the stone loses its virtue if it remains for any length of time after the death of the dragon."

Philostrates stated: "To lure dragons from their caves, seekers of the stones weave magical letters of gold into scarlet cloaks; the letters were infused with an opiate. Hunters play music in the hope of luring the dragon from its den; the opiate woven into the golden letters

THE GREEK WRESTLER MILO OF CROTON ASCRIBED HIS POWER TO ALECTORIUS

render the dragon helpless. Then the hunters rush upon him and sever the head from its body. On many an occasion the reflexes of the hunter have been dulled by those same opiates secreted in his cloak. Then the dragon has seized the hunter and drawn him into his cave."

A DEEP SLEEP

Camillus Leonardus, in *The Mirror of Stones*, writes:

"Some bold fellows in those eastern parts search out the dens of dragons, and in them they throw grass mixed with a soporific medicament, which the dragons, when they return to their dens, eat, and are thrown into a deep sleep, and in that condition their

heads are cut off, and the stone extracted. It has the rare virtue of absorbing all poisons, especially that of serpents. It also renders the possessor bold and invincible, for which reason kings of the East boast of having such a stone."

LAPIS DRACONIUS WAS SAID TO COME FROM THE HEADS OF FIERCE DRAGONS

LAPIS MEMPHITICUS

Memphiticus has been described as a round, sparkling body the size and colour of a hazelnut. Crushing the stone and taking the powder in wine or water was said to effectively deaden pain during minor surgical operations such as lancing or cauterizing.

A LOCAL ANAESTHETIC

According to the first-century pharmacist Dioscorides, a fine memphiticus powder was usually mixed with fats and oils and "applied to those parts of the body to which a surgeon was about to apply either fire or knife, for it produced insensibility to pain." Records kept by surgeons of the Roman Imperial Army have described this ointment as an effective painkiller. These records, regarded as being among the earliest referring to

YOUNG SWALLOWS WERE SAID TO BE THE SOURCE OF POTENT STONES

local anaesthetics, could easily have been lost but for the diligence of Pliny, who collected all kinds of writings.

St Isadore, Bishop of Seville, reported memphiticus as rendering men insensible to torture when it was powdered and drunk in vinegar.

SWALLOW STONE

Swallow stone (Chelidonius) is listed among those stones highly prized by the ancients, who used them for the relief of all kinds of illnesses. There were two kinds of stone – red and white – and, to be effective, they had to be taken from the maws of young swallows. It was also important that they should not be allowed to come in contact with the ground, water, or any other stone.

To relieve headaches, it was advised that the stones should be "tied in white linen and put on the man who needed them – he shall soon be better." Rolled in a yellow cloth and tied about the neck, the stones were reputed to cure jaundice and

prevent fevers. Stones of either colour were also effective against pain in the eyes, agues, temptations, goblins, incubii, herb magic, witchcraft and evil sorceries.

STRANGE DISEASES

The author of *Magical Jewels* (Joan Evans, 1922) tells us of a greeting sent by the Patriarch of Jerusalem to King Alfred of England. In it, he recommends white swallow stone as being "good against the stitch and against flying venom and against all strange diseases... You must scrape it in water and drink a large amount of it... and the stones are good to drink against strange things and if any man is in delusion, strike a spark from it in front of him and he at once becomes right."

FACT & FANTASY

ONE OF THE MOST GHOULISH MYTHICAL STONES IS KNOWN AS PIROPHOLOS, SAID TO BE LIGHTWEIGHT, BRIGHT RED AND RECOVERED FROM THE HEART OF A MAN THAT HAS DIED FROM POISONING. IT IS BELIEVED THAT THE HEART OF SUCH A MAN CANNOT BE CONSUMED BY FIRE AND THAT THE STONE PROTECTS ITS OWNER FROM LIGHTNING AND TEMPEST. THE STONE'S PRINCIPAL VIRTUE, HOWEVER, WAS TO PREVENT SUDDEN DEATH, ALTHOUGH IT DID NOT PREVENT DEATH FROM DISEASE – INSTEAD, IT CONFERRED A LINGERING DEATH.

HORN OF THE UNICORN

Although we now concede that the fabulous beast of the Middle Ages known as the unicorn was at best a figment of imagination, the so-called "horn of the unicorn" was real and tangible enough to the un-schooled because it could be seen and touched.

Sailors down the ages, drinking their ale in dock-side taverns, easily earned another tipple by telling tales of breath-taking wonders to be seen in foreign lands. The sailors of the medieval era, travelling the seas of the then known world, brought what they claimed was magical unicorn horn home to Europe and all who saw the horn marvelled at it.

THIRST FOR KNOWLEDGE

The exploits of adventurers fired the imagination of the people. In their thirst for knowledge of other lands, they were only too ready to believe the sailors' theatrical stories. In particular, they took to their hearts any description of the fabulous beast that had no option but to surrender its magical horn to man.

TALES OF FABULOUS BEASTS ABOUNDED IN LOCAL TAVERNS

Coming from such a magical creature, the horn, by association, was certain to be endowed with fabulous powers. And the sailor who was fortunate enough to have acquired the horn of a unicorn exploited his find to the utmost by cutting it into many segments and selling them in the harbour tavern. In this way he made enough money to retire from the hard life endured by seafarers of those times.

PLEASING PROPORTIONS

Generally, the horn was said to have a length of about two metres. It was well proportioned, with the ratio of diameter to length giving a pleasing, straight

THE UNICORN HELD A UNIQUE PLACE IN THE PUBLIC IMAGINATION

ROYAL FAVOUR

Pendants of this type are often recorded in the inventories of kings and dukes, and others who could afford to purchase such a treasure. In 1388, the king of France possessed a "touch", as did the dukes of Burgundy in 1456. Henry VI of England owned one "to put in our drink", while Henry VII had "a unicorn's bone and a serpent's tongue hanged by a cheyne." In an inventory of Mary, Queen of Scots' possessions is "a unicorn's horn garnished with gold and attached to a chain of gold" (Evans, *Magic of Jewels*, 1922) – although it failed to save her from execution.

A sacred image would sometimes be made from a piece of unicorn horn. Ivan the Terrible of Russia, claimed that his royal staff was made from a "unicorn's horn... garnished with verie fare diomondes, rubies, saphiers, emeralls & other precious stone that are rich in value."

Some members of the aristocracy, mistrustful of those around them, would have a segment of the horn fixed in raised claw settings at the bottom of a drinking goblet. The royal throne of Denmark, made in the seventeenth-century, consists almost completely of unicorn horn (narwhal horn). This throne was meant to call to mind the thrones of the ancient Danish chieftains and the inherant magic of the horn.

An excerpt from the will of Sir Nathaniel Bacon (1614) reads:

"I give to all my three daughters the jewel of Unicorn's horn, according to their mother's direction, that each may challenge the use thereof when needs require and my wife may have the use thereof when she needs..."

shape. In reality, the horn of these far-fetched tales was the left-hand spirally twisted ivory tusk of an Arctic Whale – the Narwhal.

The commonest use for many gemstones and other materials was as touchstones. To this end, a segment of supposed unicorn horn was set in a gold frame and either attached to a particular goblet by a chain of gold, or worn as a pendant at mealtimes. Dipping the horn into the wine, or touching the food with it, freed and made safe the user from possible contamination by poison.

4 Gemstone Superstitions

ANNIVERSARIES

MONDAY'S child is fair of face;
TUESDAY'S child is full of grace;
WEDNESDAY'S child is full of woe;
THURSDAY'S child has far to go;
FRIDAY'S child is loving and giving;
SATURDAY'S child works hard for a living;
And the child that is born on the SABBATH day
is Bonny and Blythe and Good and Gay.

TRADITIONAL RHYME

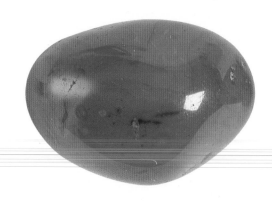

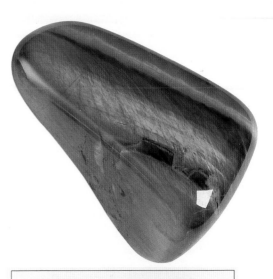

G ems have long been associated with various anniversaries, and are believed to bring good fortune to those born at a certain time of year.

GEMSTONES OF THE ZODIAC

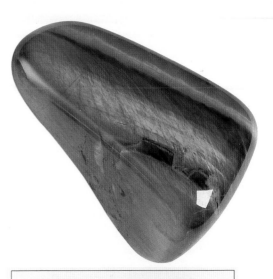

FACT & FANTASY

WEARING GEMSTONES AND METALS THAT ARE UNDER THE INFLUENCE OF THEIR TUTELARY PLANETS HAS BEEN PRACTISED FOR MANY CENTURIES IN THE VARIOUS COUNTRIES OF THE MIDDLE AND FAR EAST. THIS PRACTICE DID NOT REACH EUROPE UNTIL ABOUT AD1500.

Aquarius	January 20–February 18	Garnet/Turquoise
Pisces	February 19–March 20	Amethyst
Aries	March 21–April 20	Bloodstone/Carnelian
Taurus	April 21–May 20	Rose Quartz
Gemini	May 21–June 20	Citrine/Tiger's Eye
Cancer	June 21–July 20	Emerald/Chrysoprase
Leo	July 21–August 21	Rock Crystal/Onyx
Virgo	August 22–September 22	Carnelian
Libra	September 23–October 22	Peridot/Jacinth
Scorpio	October 23–November 22	Aquamarine
Sagittarius	November 23–December 20	Topaz
Capricorn	December 21–January 19	Ruby

GEMSTONES FOR A BIRTH MONTH

January	Zircon
February	Amethyst
March	Jasper/Bloodstone
April	Sapphire/Diamond
May	Agate
June	Emerald/Pearl
July	Onyx/Turquoise
August	Carnelian/Moonstone
September	Peridot
October	Opal/Aquamarine
November	Topaz
December	Ruby

WEDDING ANNIVERSARIES

Many people in parts of Asia and the Far East are strongly superstitious and will not embark on any venture of importance without consulting their local astrologer. He is required to predict the most propitious day and time to embark on all kinds of undertakings, including getting engaged or married, and will even comment on the likely compatibility of prospective couples.

He will advise on the gem to wear for different anniversaries, for how long the stone should be worn and whether it should touch the skin if worn in a ring. This practice filtered into Europe and has now been confined to a list of materials from which gifts are to be made for each of the following wedding anniversaries.

1.	Paper	15.	Rock Crystal
2.	Calico	16.	Topaz
3.	Linen	17.	Amethyst
4.	Silk	18.	Garnet
5.	Wood	19.	Zircon
6.	Candy	20.	China
7.	Floral	23.	Sapphire
8.	Leather	25.	Silver
9.	Straw	30.	Pearl
10.	Tin	35.	Coral
11.	Copper	40.	Ruby
12.	Agate	50.	Gold
13.	Moonstone	55.	Emerald
14.	Moss Agate		

And for the 60th anniversary... Diamond.

HEALING STONES

As we have seen throughout this book, many stones have been credited with the power either to cure or relieve certain ailments. Physicians of past centuries often recommended that stones should be finely powdered, mixed with fruit juice and syrup and taken internally. It was also advised that healing stones could be strung together and worn as a necklaces.

The following list has been drawn up from the writings of Theophrastus, Pliny, Dioscorides, Galen, Camillus Leonardus, Cantimpre, Beauvais, Dr Johann Schroder, Dr William Rowland, and many others. Only those stones which are identifiable today as gems have been included.

EVERY GEM HAS BEEN CREDITED WITH A SPECIAL HEALING POWER

ILLNESS	GEMSTONE
Ague	Sapphire
Allepo boils	Agate
Apoplexy	Lapis Lazuli
Arthritis	Amber
Asthma	Amber, Jade
Bad temper	Carnelian, Zircon
Biliousness	Jade (purple/yellow)
Bladder problems	Bloodstone, Flint, Haematite, Diamond
Blood purification	Jade, Lapis Lazuli, Coral
Boils	Agate, Sapphire
Bone problems	Jade
Cataract	Sapphire
Catarrh	Amber
Chest and Lungs	Agate, Amber, Carnelian, Jade
Cholera	Malachite
Colic	Coral, Rock Crystal

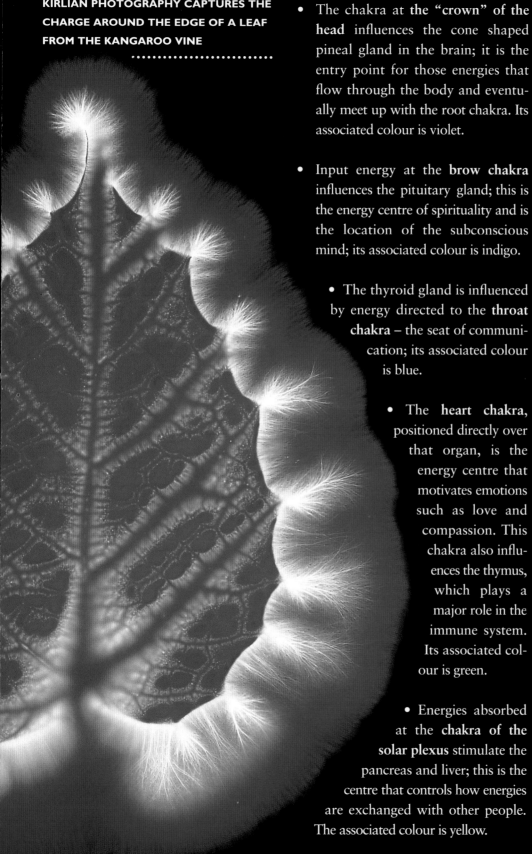

- The chakra at **the "crown" of the head** influences the cone shaped pineal gland in the brain; it is the entry point for those energies that flow through the body and eventually meet up with the root chakra. Its associated colour is violet.

- Input energy at the **brow chakra** influences the pituitary gland; this is the energy centre of spirituality and is the location of the subconscious mind; its associated colour is indigo.

- The thyroid gland is influenced by energy directed to the **throat chakra** – the seat of communication; its associated colour is blue.

- The **heart chakra,** positioned directly over that organ, is the energy centre that motivates emotions such as love and compassion. This chakra also influences the thymus, which plays a major role in the immune system. Its associated colour is green.

- Energies absorbed at the **chakra of the solar plexus** stimulate the pancreas and liver; this is the centre that controls how energies are exchanged with other people. The associated colour is yellow.

- The **chakra of the spleen or lower abdomen** exerts its influence on the spleen, the liver and adrenals. It is the area where "gut instincts" are said to be situated. Its associated colour is orange.

- The **"root" chakra, at the base of the spine,** controls physical vitality. The endocrine glands influenced by this chakra are the gonads, and the associated colour is red.

TALISMANS OF CHILDBIRTH

"I am told by my Lady that in time of labour it [eagle stone] hould be tyed to the thigh to cause an easy delivery."

A CERTAIN "SIR STREYNSHAM"

The wonder that people feel at the birth of a new life does not diminish over the centuries – and neither do the attendant fears and worries about pregnancy and delivery. So, it is hardly surprising that talismans have become particularly associated with this difficult time. A catalogue of a few of the ancient talismans of childbirth follows; you will find more under the individual stones in previous chapters.

PLINY RECOMMENDED THAT "EAGLE STONES" BE WORN DURING PREGNANCY
....

EAGLE STONE
(also Ethices, Endes, Aquileus, Praegnus)

The most widely known and sought-after talisman of childbirth was the Aetites Lapis or Eagle Stone, supposedly found in eagles' nests. Pliny (*Historia Naturalis*) describes four varieties and says "that they are usually found in pairs, as male and female stones. Without them the eagles cannot produce their young."

PREGNANT STONE

Eagle stones are said to be hollow and to contain a detached stone-within-a-stone – the "callimus" – that rattles when the stone is shaken. It was this loose callimus that gave rise to the idea that the stone was pregnant, and so it was given the name '"praegnus".

AID TO BIRTH

Pliny writes that the stones must be "wrapped in the skins of animals that have been sacrificed and then worn as amulets by women or four footed creatures during pregnancy so as to prevent miscarriage. They must not be removed except at the moment of delivery; otherwise there will be a prolapse of delivery. On the other hand, if they were not removed during delivery a birth would not take place." (*Historia Naturalis*.)

During the seventeenth and eighteenth centuries, the stones were highly popular and their owners regularly loaned them to friends and neighbours when necessary. Midwives usually recommended that the stone be kept in a little silk bag, so that it could be worn about the neck during pregnancy and tied to the thigh during labour.

LAPIS LAZULI

Lapis lazuli (see pages 56–57) was burned in furnaces to produce the blue artists's pigment, ultramarine. Physicians would also add the pigment to a soothing medicinal syrup called Alkermes Syrup, made from the fruit of a particular tree that grows in France and Spain.

This syrup was prescribed by physicians for women experiencing a difficult labour; "it gives great comfort", according to Dr William Rowland during the 1600s... "but it must be removed near the time of delivery lest it keep up the child." Today, in Macedonia, an amulet of lapis lazuli is carried by expectant mothers to prevent a miscarriage.

THUNDER STONE

Technically, "thunder stones" are actually axe-heads and hammer-heads chipped from flint (see pages 72–73) by Stone-age man. According to certain Nordic folktales, these assisted women in labour if generous measures of ale were poured over the stone and were then given to the expectant mother to drink.

ST ALBANS STONE

William Jones (1880) writes that, at the construction of a shrine dedicated to their patron saint by Geoffrey, abbot of St Albans, it was decided that a certain stone – the gift of King Ethelred – was to be placed within the shrine.

"On it," says Jones, "was carved an image, as of one in ragged clothes, holding a spear in one hand, with a 'snake' winding itself up on it. In the other hand it bore a small boy bearing a buckler [a small round shield]. At the feet of the image was an eagle with wings expanded and lifted up."

This precious stone was so large that a man could not grasp it in his hand. It was said to help women in childbirth and was taken to their homes at the time of delivery. It may be that the stone was actually a piece of onyx.

CARNELIAN

According to Drs Schroeder and Rowlands, a Carnelian "bound to the belly keeps up the birth." (See page 30.)

EMERALD

For its colour, emeralds have been linked with the goddess of nature, Diana (Artemis to the Greeks), who is also considered the guardian of women (see pages 40–43). And so emeralds, for their connection with Diana, are credited with the power to encourage easy childbirth. According to Drs Schroeder

CARNELIAN WAS SAID TO BE EFFECTIVE WHEN "BOUND TO THE BELLY"

and Rowland, an emerald amulet: "helped the birth if bound to the hip, and holds it in if bound to the belly."

CAT'S EYES
(Cymophane or Quartz)

In Asia, particularly India, cat's eye stones (see pages 32–33) are reputed to bring a safe delivery in cases of protracted labour. The stone is tied to the hair of the mother-to-be.

CAT'S EYES ARE SAID TO BRING AID IN A LENGTHY DELIVERY

THE EVIL EYE

"If thine eye be evil, thy whole body shall be full of darkness"

NEW TESTAMENT (MATTHEW)

From earliest times, those who saw themselves as guardians of the people's morals cautioned against envy and envious looks. Out of that grew a belief that some people had a glance so malevolent that it blighted whatever or whoever it happened to light upon, bringing ill fortune, illness – even death.

This forceful superstition took root in every civilization, especially in lands along the Mediterranean, and talismans that had the power to deflect, and sometimes return, those evil-minded glances were soon highly sought after.

Nowhere is this belief more persistent than in Italy, where the Evil Eye is called *jettatura* or *mal occhio*. In southern Italy, a legend persists that talismans carved from red coral will protect against such glances. These talismans are in the form of a hand, with only the index and little finger extended – a fully extended hand is known as the "hand of Fatima".

OTHER FOLKLORE

The folklore of other civilizations has various versions on this theme. Ancient Babylonians were fearful of a malign female spirit named Labastu, said to be the bringer of disease. Babylonian texts have described how explicit instructions were given to the populace on how to overcome her influence by making eye agate amulets.

For many centuries, horn shaped amulets have been regarded as an efficient means of gaining protection from the Evil Eye; and in many countries they are still regarded as such. The people of the Abruzzi region of Italy still use red coral amulets in the shape of a crescent moon, which is similar to a pair of horns, and call on St Donato to shield them from the Evil Eye. An image of St Donato, made from clay or plaster, is placed between the "horns" of the crescent. Horns of oxen, and even boars' tusks, are often seen set over the entrances of many Saharan Arabian dwellings.

THE EYE OF RA

In common with many people living along the Mediterranean coast, the ancient Egyptians believed themselves to be potential victims of a blighting glance. They often employed a stylized eye of Ra, Horus or Osiris, to overcome its evil influence.

And along parts of the Mediterranean coast today, many believe that all men with light blue eyes and fair hair – a rarity in

THE DISTINCTIVE HAND TALISMAN
SAID TO DEFLECT EVIL GLANCES

this area – possess the gift of the Evil Eye, especially if the men are also beardless.

PROTECTOR OF WOMEN

The women of lands such as Lebanon and Syria often wear strings of blue beads as a protective measure and beads of the finest blue turquoise are used as talismans for the same purpose in Turkey. "Eye agates" have also been seen to hold this power – this is black or brown agate that has been polished in such a way that a white ring becomes visible towards the centre of the stone.

During the 1850s, a thriving handicraft industry became established in Idar-Oberstein, Germany, producing just such stones. They were exported in great quantities to the Sudan, where a stone with a white ring surrounding the central "iris" is still regarded as the symbol of the eye, able to deflect an evil glance.

FACT & FANTASY

THE BELIEF IN CORAL IS AN ANCIENT ONE. GRATIUS (FIRST CENTURY AD; A CONTEMPORARY OF THE POET OVID), WROTE OF HIS FIRM BELIEF THAT WEARING CORAL PLEASED THE GODS, WHO THEN BROKE THE SPELLS CAST BY ENVIOUS EYES.

THE EYE OF RA WAS A POTENT FORCE FOR THE ANCIENT EGYPTIANS

LEGENDS OF THE EAST

"We who dwell in this palace have lived in luxury for many years. Now famine is upon us and we have ground pearls into flour instead of wheat, but to no avail. Our King has slain a million heroes and ruled over thousands of provinces but when the Angel of Death approached us he was powerless"

H. E. GOLDING, THE *BOOK OF LEGENDS*

KING SOLOMON AND THE QUEEN OF SHEBA

••

Nowhere in the world has belief in the mysterious powers of gemstones taken hold more strongly than in the Middle and Far East, and especially the Mediterranean lands. All these areas have magical tales of gemstones to relate, many of which trace their origins back to the supposed writings of King Solomon.

THE GOLDEN PLACE

Golding's *Book of Legends* tells of a sorcerer who sat upon his magic carpet and ordered the wind to carry him to the remotest part of the land. For seven days and seven nights he journeyed, until he spied far beneath him a magnificent golden castle. The sorcerer ordered the carpet to take him down. He attempted to enter the castle but could find no door, for deep sands had piled right up to the highest ramparts. And so the sorcerer ordered the wind to blow away the sands and an entrance was revealed. Fixed to the door was the inscription seen at the head of this article.

THE GUARDIAN ANGEL

According to an Arabic tradition, Ishmael, by command of the Most High, was ordered to rebuild the Kaaba – the splendid stone building situated within the Great Mosque of Mecca.

When the builders had almost completed their task, the Archangel Gabriel brought them a large gemstone and told them to place it in front of the building, a metre or so off the ground and near the door. He told them that this stone had originally been the Guardian Angel appointed to watch over Adam and Eve in the Garden of Eden. Because the angel had failed to protect the first man and woman from the serpent's wiles, he had been turned into a gemstone and thrown out of Paradise, until retrieved by Gabriel.

THE KISSES OF THE SINFUL

When the stone was given to Abraham and Ishmael it was a jacinth (zircon) of "dazzling whiteness" but, it is said, it has now become blackened by the kisses of sinful pilgrims endeavouring to cleanse their souls. Legend has it that when the trumpet is sounded at the Resurrection, the stone will revert to its previous form of an Angel and bear witness for those who have performed the sacred rites of pilgrimage to Mecca.

THE QUEEN OF SHEEBA

The legendary Queen of Sheba was somewhat sceptical of the great King Solomon's powers as a benign sorcerer. When she sent an ambassador with many gifts for the King, she attempted to test his powers.

Among the gifts was a gold crown, encrusted with many precious stones and pearls; five hundred bars of gold; a golden casket containing an un-drilled pearl; and an onyx drilled with a crooked hole. Other gifts included five hundred boy slaves and five hundred girl slaves – all of whom were dressed alike. The tests were to drill the pearl; thread the onyx and separate the boys from the girls.

SPECIAL POWERS

Using his powers as a sorcerer, the King commanded a special worm to drill the pearl and another to carry a thread through the crooked hole in the onyx. The separation of the five hundred boys from the five hundred girls was more by observation than by sorcery. King Soloman noticed that the boys drank water from a goatskin held high, while the girls drank only from goblets.

OYSTER SHELLS – THE 'MOTHERS' OF PEARLS

THE LEGEND OF PRESTER JOHN

Minstrels, troubadours and wandering players, journeying through the well-travelled highways of medieval Europe, were often requested to end their play or recital with the singing of at least one fabulous legend about the magical figure of Prester John and his fabulous domain.

Prester (meaning an elder of the early Christian church) John was perceived by the West as a mysterious Indian priest-king, said to have reigned sometime in the twelfth century, who showed himself to his subjects just three times a year.

....

PRESTER JOHN, MEDIEVAL CHIEF OF A CHRISTIAN TRIBE

THE KINGDOM OF PENTOXERE

Pentoxere was the name of the kingdom ruled by John, of which the principal city was called Nise, and many wondrous descriptions of that kingdom reached Europe. Prester John had under his rule over seventy provinces, and each was ruled by a king who had other kings under him, all subservient to Prester John.

This vast land was wealthy beyond all imagination, but merchants were advised not to travel there, for the journey was long and arduous, and travel by sea was exceedingly dangerous. The danger lay in the fact that rocks with the power to draw iron to them lay off the coast of Pentoxere, and so only ships put together without nails could sail there.

AN ISLAND OF BUSHES AND TREES

Sir John Mandeville claims to have made the journey and described what looked like an island of trees and bushes. Seamen told him, he said, that the trees and bushes were growing from items of cargo carried by ships that had been drawn to the islands because of the iron built into them.

The great prize for all who managed to reach Pentoxere were opportunities to obtain gems of such size and quality that dishes, bowls, cups and all sorts of other artefacts were made from them.

THE FORGED LETTERS

John was said to have sent letters to Manuel of Constantinople and to Frederick, the Roman Emperor. In these letters – now believed to be forgeries –

he described his Palace as follows:

"The palace in which our supereminency resides, is built after the pattern of the castle built by the Apostle Thomas for the Indian King Gundoforus. Ceilings, joists, and architrave are of Sethym wood; the roof of Ebony, which can never catch fire. Over the gable of the palace are, at the extremities, two golden apples in which are two carbuncles (cabochon-cut garnets), so that the gold may shine by day and the carbuncles by night. The great gates are of Sardius, with the horn of the horned snake in-wrought, so that no one can bring poison within.

STROLLING PLAYERS OFTEN TOLD FABULOUS TALES OF PRESTER JOHN

"The other portals are of Ebony. The windows are of Crystal. The tables are partly of gold, partly of Amethyst, and the columns supporting the tables are partly of Ivory, partly of Amethyst...

"The court in which we watch the jousting is paved with Onyx in order to increase the courage of the combatants and turn aside the wicked eye; this court being reserved and set aside for judicial ordeal combat."

Before the palace stood a mirror, the ascent to which consisted of five and twenty steps of Porphry and Serpentine. Fabulous jewels encrusted the frame of this mirror, with a warning that 3,000 armed men stand guard over it. When John looked in the mirror, he could view all the lands under his rule.

TRAVELLER'S TALES

In his *Travels*, Sir John Mandeville adds to the colourful descriptions of the palace:

"The borders... of the gates are of Ivory. All the tables on which the men eat are of Emerald, some of Amethyst, and some of gold full of precious stones.

"Of the steps approaching his throne where he sits at meat, one is of Onyx, another Crystal, and another Green Jasper, another Amethyst, another Sardonyx, another Coral and the seventh and highest step on which he rests his feet when at meat, is of Chrysolite. All these steps are bordered with fine gold, set full of Pearls and other Precious Stones on the sides and edges.

"The sides of the seat of his throne are of Emeralds, and bordered full nobly with gold, and dubbed with other precious stones and great pearls. All the pillars in his chamber are of fine gold with precious stones, and with many Carbuncles, which give great light by night to all people. The frame of his bed is of fine Sapphire blended with gold which retains his chastity and makes him sleep well." [Note: In antiquity, sapphire was the name used for Lapis lazuli.]

MAGICAL RINGS

Jewelled rings have often been worn as talismans, by rich and poor alike, all over the world. What follows is just a small selection of the tales surrounding some especially powerful rings.

THE SILVER RING OF GALEN

Numbered among the most famous of Greek philosophers and physicians is Klaudios Galenos. Galen, as he is generally called, was revered for many centuries as the supreme medical authority. He is believed to have worn a silver ring set with a carnelian, engraved with the figure of a man wearing a bundle of herbs suspended from his neck. Legend has it that the wearer of this kind of ring was given the intuition and ability to diagnose illness and disability, as well as the power to stop a haemorrhage when the wound was touched with the stone.

ELEAZER'S HERBAL RING

In AD 40, Titus destroyed the famous Temple in Jerusalem and most of the population was enslaved and taken to Rome to be sold. A notable captive was the Jewish historian and philosopher Josephus Flavius.

During antiquity, much use was made of the mandrake root by physicians and magicians all over the then known world. Josephus Flavius is recorded as having witnessed a man, whom he knew as Eleazer, giving a demonstration of exorcism.

He goes on to say that the manner of the cure was to secrete in his ring a piece of mandrake root, of the sort used and prescribed by King Solomon. Having put the ring to the nostrils, the patient fell unconscious. He continues:

THE FAMOUS GREEK PHYSICIAN CLAUDIUS GALEN WORE A RING OF CARNELIAN

"He commanded the demon to return to him no more, making mention of Solomon and reciting those incantations Solomon had composed. And Eleazer wishing to show that he had such a power, caused to be set a basin of water a little way off and commanded the demon, as he went out of the man, to overturn it and so let the people know that he had left the man."

THE RING OF SALUS

Numbered among the many deities invoked by the Romans was Salus, whose temple was dedicated to Welfare and Safety. She was also known as Hygiea, the goddess of health and the daughter of Asclepius. Devotees of Salus usually wore what is known today as the Salus Ring, believed to keep them in good health and bring their daily undertakings to successful conclusions.

The form of this item of jewellery was that of a signet ring, and the bezel or signet part was circular. On the outer circumference was engraved a curious emblem called a "curoboros" – a magic circle into which nothing outside could enter and from which nothing inside could escape. This circle was usually shown engraved as a snake swallowing its own tail. The centre of the ring was engraved with a pentacle, between the arms of which were letters or characters prescribed by the priests of the order.

RHINOCEROUS RINGS

A superstition arose in the Far East, particularly in China and India, that the perfect aphrodisiac was powdered rhinoceros horn. This belief was also imported into Europe by surgeons to the Roman legions, and one Roman physician prescribed finger rings fashioned from the hoof of a rhinoceros to banish nightmares and cure nervous complaints.

Medicinally, the horn was used in preparations prescribed for the relief of epilepsy, paralysis and labour pains. Signet rings set with a piece cut from the horn of the animal were credited with power to overcome the effects of subtle poison.

SNAKE RINGS

Rings with snake symbols have also been thought to be powerful talismans. Snake cults have been traced back to before the Bronze Age. The Minoans adopted snake worship into their religious and cultural ceremonies and it was accepted by the Greeks and Romans. As the snake grows, it sloughs its skin and becomes rejuvenated, and so it has become associated with rejuvenation, longevity and wisdom. Because of its phallic shape, it is also associated with sexuality and fertility.

....

A SEAL RING OF RED JASPER THAT BELONGED TO MARK ANTONY

GOOD VIBRATIONS

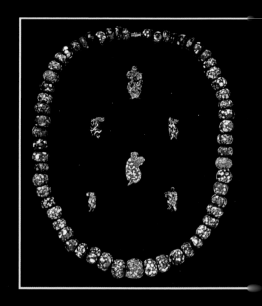

"... So much is true, that gems have fine spirits, as appears by their splendour, and therefore may operate, by consent, on the spirits of men, to strengthen and exhilarate them. As for their particular properties, no credit can be given to them. But it is manifest that light, above all things, rejoices the spirits of men; and, probably, varied light has the same effect, with greater novelty; which may be one cause why precious stones exhilarate"

FRANCIS BACON, WRITER (1561–1626)

Much has been written on the supernatural powers and the healing "vibrations" and energies of crystals and gemstones. Anselmus Boetius de Boot, author of a most important lapidary entitled *Gemmarum et Lapidum Historia* (published in 1636), believed that, as products of nature, gemstones in themselves did not have the power to create supernatural effect. He goes on to say that:

"any such that may appear to be accomplished through them are due not to them but to God or to a good or evil spirit subject to him who uses them only as an instrument."

MAGIC, RELIGION AND SCIENCE

Over 2,000 years ago, Plato devised an interesting theory. This theory suggested that decayed matter became gradually converted into perfect gemstones as a result of influences exerted by the stars and planets. The theory appears to have been eagerly adopted by ancient astrologers and magical diviners who devised systems to foretell the future for their clients.

Gnostics and other religious groups used gemstones in their ceremonies; countless physicians used them for their supposed healing forces; and modern day scientists employ gemstones and other crystals – natural and man-made – to generate laser beams with which they are able to measure small objects on the moon with great accuracy.

VIBRATIONS

There are some who will argue that, as all matter is constructed of

ally vibrates in harmony with the movement of electrons revolving in their designated orbits around the nuclei of those atoms.

It would follow then, they say, that, when the vibrations within a gemstone are in harmony with the particular vibrations of the wearer, they complement each other. This will then ensure a state of well-being. Conversely, when the peaks and troughs of the vibrations are out of phase (crests of one set of vibrations opposing the troughs of the other set) they cancel each other out and there is no effect.

Also, many believe that, when the vibrations from the stone are stronger and vibrating in a different plane, the stone exerts its individual nature – which in some stones may be benign and in others malev-olent.

CAN THE LIGHT TRAVELLING THROUGH A PRISM (LEFT), HAVE A HEALING EFFECT, OR (INSET) ARE THERE INVISIBLE ENERGY FORCES AT WORK IN THE AMULETS AND NECKLACES WE WEAR?

5 *Ready Reference*

GEMSTONE AUTHORITIES

THE ANCIENTS

PLATO

This great Greek philosopher originated a theory that stars and planets converted decayed and decaying matter into the most perfect of gemstones, which then came under the influence of those same stars and planets.

THE PHILOSOPHER PLATO 427-347 BC
THEORIZED ON THE SOURCE OF GEMS

THEOPHRASTUS

A pupil of Aristotle. Later recognized as one of the major Greek philosophers. He wrote many treatises on gemstones, in which he divided stones into male and female. From this arose a fanciful theory that gems were able to breed.

PLINY (The Elder)

Pliny was once a commander of the Roman cavalry in Germany. At a later time he was appointed by Emperor Vespasian to command the Roman fleet stationed in the Bay of Naples, which was positioned there in order to suppress piracy. During his retirement he wrote the 37-volume encyclopedia, *Historia Naturalis*, dedicated to the Emperor Titus.

The influence of Pliny's work diminished after Niccolo Leoniceno's work *De Erroribus Plinii* was published in Ferrara in 1492. At the end of the seventeenth century, *Historia Naturalis* was no longer consulted by scientists and was consigned to the shelves of literary museums.

DIOSCORIDES

Wrote *Materia Medica*, which became the textbook of pharmacy for more than 1600 years. The fifth volume describes over 200 stones to be used medicinally.

CLAUDIUS GALEN (Klaudios Galenos)

This second-century scholar was considered the most famous of Greek physicians. For hundreds of years his texts were the supreme medical authority. Modern pharmacists still refer to their bulk medicines as "Galenicals".

EPIPHANIUS

Bishop of Constantia. Wrote the influential *Sixteenth Book of Etymologie*.

ST ISADORE

One-time Bishop of Seville. He wrote *Etymologiae* during the seventh century.

THE MIDDLE AGES

MARBODE
Bishop of Rennes between 1067 and 1081. Wrote a notable lapidary in Latin hexameters. Pliny and Damigeron are believed to be Marbode's principal sources of reference.

....

GREEK PHYSICIAN GALEN 131-200 AD DETAILED USES FOR GEMSTONES

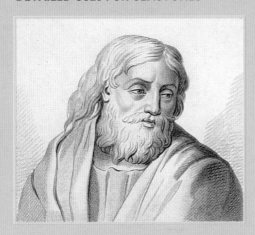

ALBERTUS MAGNUS
Bishop of Ratisbon during the thirteenth century. Author of *Secrets de Virtus des Herbes, Pierres et Bestes*.

THOMAS de CANTIMPRE
Thirteenth-century author of *De Natura Rarum*. He was, at one time, a pupil of Albertus Magnus.

VINCENT de BEAUVAIS
A preaching friar; wrote *Speculum Maius*.

BARTHOLOMAEUS
Wrote a handbook on the properties of gems entitled *De Proprietatibus Rerum*, for use by teaching friars and monks.

SIR JOHN MANDEVILLE
Author of *Travels and Voyages*, first written in medieval French in the 1300s. Translated into modern French by J. S. del Sotto and published in Vienna, 1861.

THE 1600S AND 1700S

CAMILLUS LEONARDUS
Author of *Speculum Lapidum*, published in Venice in 1502. The book was dedicated to Cesare Borgia, to whom he was physician. Translated and published in London (1750) as *The Mirror of Stones*.

REGINALD SCOT
Wrote *Discoverie of Witchcraft* in 1584.

JEROME CARDAN
Wrote *De Gemmis et Coloribus* in 1587.

SIR JAMES HARRINGTON
Author of *Oceana* in 1607 and translator of an old medical treatise written in verse entitled *Schola Salernitana*.

ANSELMUS BOETIUS de BOOT
Wrote *Gemmarium et Lapidum Historia* (Published at Lyons, 1636). "Precious stones produce effects which challenge wonder and admiration."

THOMAS NICHOLS
Wrote *The History of Precious Stones*, 1652 and *The Faithful Lapidary*, 1659.

DR JOHANNES SCHROEDER
Wrote *The Complete Chemical Dispensatory*, 1669.

DR W. ROWLAND
Translated Schroeder's *Dispensatory* from Latin to English. He advised physicians to devise methods for their own practice "not withstanding the envy of this age against invention".

THE 1800S

PROFESSOR FRANCIS BARRETT
Wrote *The Celestial Intelligencer*, 1801, about the supernatural properties of metals, gemstones and herbs.

RAJAH SOURINDRO MOHUN TAGORE
Wrote *A Treatise on Gems* in 1879. Describes the magical and healing properties of gems in Indian folklore.

....

PLINIUS (PLINY) THE ELDER, 23-79 AD

A-Z GEM DATA CHART

This chart details the basic facts and figures of the standard, well-known inorganic and organic stones – many of which have been featured in this book. You will find more about crystal structures at the beginning of the book.

SG = Specific Gravity; RI = Refractive Index.

GEM	COMPOSITION	CRYSTAL STRUCTURE	HARDNESS	SG	RI
Agate (Chalcedony)	Silicon dioxide	Trigonal/Hexagonal	7	2.61	1.53–1.54
Amber	Plant resins	Amorphous	2½	1.08	1.54–1.55
Amethyst (Quartz)	Silicon dioxide	Trigonal/Hexagonal	7	2.65	1.54–1.55
Apatite	Calcium phosphate	Hexagonal	5	3.20	1.63–1.64
Aquamarine (Beryl)	Aluminium beryllium silicate	Hexagonal/Trigonal	7½	2.69	1.57–1.58
Azurite	Copper carbonate hydroxycarbonate	Monoclinic	3½	3.77	1.73–1.84
Bloodstone (Chalcedony)	Silicon dioxide	Trigonal/Hexagonal	7	2.61	1.53–1.54
Smoky Quartz	Silicon dioxide	Trigonal/Hexagonal	7	2.65	1.54–1.55
Calcite	Calcium carbonate	Trigonal/Hexagonal	3	2.71	1.48–1.66
Carnelian (Chalcedony)	Silicon dioxide	Trigonal/Hexagonal	7	2.61	1.53–1.54
Chatoyant Quartz (incl. Cat's Eye; Tiger's Eye)	Silicon dioxide	Trigonal/Hexagonal	7	2.65	1.54–1.55
Citrine (Quartz)	Silicon dioxide	Trigonal/Hexagonal	7	2.65	1.54–1.55
Chrysoberyl	Beryllium aluminium oxide	Orthorhombic	8½	3.71	1.74–1.75

GEM	COMPOSITION	CRYSTAL STRUCTURE	HARDNESS	SG	RI
Chrysoprase/ (Chalcedony)	Silicon dioxide	Trigonal/Hexagonal	7	2.61	1.53–1.54
Coral	Calcium carbonate or conchiolin	Hexagonal/ Microcrystalline	3	2.68	1.49–1.66
Diamond	Carbon	Cubic	10	3.52	2.42
Emerald (Beryl)	Aluminium beryllium silicate	Hexagonal/Trigonal	7½	2.71	1.57–1.58
Fire Agate (Chalcedony)	Silicon dioxide	Trigonal/Hexagonal	7	2.61	1.53–1.54

GARNET					
Almandine	Iron aluminium silicate	Cubic	7½	4.00	1.76–1.83
Green Grossular	Calcium aluminium silicate	Cubic	7	3.6	1.73–1.74
Hessonite (Grossular) "Cinnamon stone"	Calcium aluminium silicate	Cubic	7¼	3.65	1.73–1.75
Pink Grossular	Calcium aluminium silicate	Cubic	7	3.49	1.69–1.73
Pyrope	Magnesium aluminium silicate	Cubic	7½	3.80	1.72–1.76
Spessartine	Manganese aluminium silicate	Cubic	7	4.16	1.79–1.81
Uvarovite	Calcium chromium silicate	Cubic	7½	3.77	1.86–1.87
Andradite	Calcium iron silicate	Cubic	6½	3.85	1.85–1.89

GEM	COMPOSITION	CRYSTAL STRUCTURE	HARDNESS	SG	RI
Gypsum/ alabaster	Hydrated calcium sulphate	Monoclinic	2	2.32	1.52–1.53
Hematite	Iron oxide	Trigonal/Hexagonal	6½	4.95–5.16	2.94–3.22

GEM	COMPOSITION	CRYSTAL STRUCTURE	HARDNESS	SG	RI
Heliodor (Beryl)	Aluminium beryllium silicate	Hexagonal/Trigonal	7½	2.65–2.75	1.57–1.60
JADE					
Jadeite	Sodium, aluminium silicate	Monoclinic	7	3.33	1.66–1.68
Nephrite	Calcium magnesium iron silicate	Monoclinic	6½	2.96	1.61–1.63
Jet	Type of lignite	Amorphous	2¼	1.33	1.64–1.68
Lapis lazuli	Rock containing lazurite and other minerals	Varies	5½	2.80	1.50
Malachite	Hydrated copper carbonate	Monoclinic	4	3.80 (on average)	1.85
Milky Quartz	Silicon dioxide	Trigonal/Hexagonal	7	2.65	1.54–1.55
Moonstone (Orthoclase)	Potassium aluminium silicate	Monoclinic	6	2.57	1.52–1.53
Obsidian	Mainly silicon	Amorphous	5	2.35	1.48–1.51
Onyx	Silicon dioxide	Trigonal/Hexagonal	7	2.61	1.53–1.54
Pearl	Calcium carbonate, conchiolin and water	Orthorhombic	3–4	2.71	1.53–1.68
Opal	Hydrous silicon dioxide	Amorphous	6	2.10	1.37–1.47
Peridot (gem quality olivine)	Magnesium iron silicate	Orthorhombic	6½	3.34	1.64–1.69
Pyrite	Iron sulphide	Cubic	6½	5–5.2	Over 1.81
Rock crystal (Quartz)	Silicon dioxide	Trigonal/Hexagonal	7	2.65	1.54–1.55
Rose quartz	Silicon dioxide	Trigonal/Hexagonal	7	2.65	1.54–1.55
Ruby (Corundum)	Aluminium oxide	Trigonal/Hexagonal	9	4.00	1.76–1.77

GEM	COMPOSITION	CRYSTAL STRUCTURE	HARDNESS	SG	RI
SAPPHIRE					
Sapphire (Corundum)	Aluminium oxide	Trigonal/Hexagonal	9	4.00	1.76–1.77
Colourless	Aluminium oxide	Trigonal	9	4.00	1.76–1.77
Green	Aluminium oxide	Trigonal	9	4.00	1.76–1.77
Pink	Aluminium oxide	Trigonal	9	4.00	1.76–1.77
Yellow	Aluminium oxide	Trigonal	9	4.00	1.76–1.77
Serpentine	Basic magnesium silicate	Monoclinic hydroxysilicate	5	2.60	1.55–1.56
Shell	Calcium carbonate	Various	2½	1.30	1.53–1.69
Spinel	Magnesium, aluminium oxide	Cubic	8	3.60	1.71–1.73
Topaz	Aluminium fluorohydroxysilicate	Orthorhombic	8	3.54	1.62–1.63
TOURMALINE					
Achroite	Complex borosilicate	Trigonal	7½	3.06	1.62–1.64
Dravite	Complex borosilicate	Trigonal	7½	3.06	1.61–1.63
Green and Yellow	Complex borosilicate	Trigonal	7½	3.06	1.62–1.64
Indicolite	Complex borosilicate	Trigonal	7½	3.06	1.62–1.64
Rubellite	Complex borosilicate	Trigonal	7½	3.06	1.62–1.64
Schorl	Complex borosilicate	Trigonal	7½	3.06	1.62–1.67
Watermelon Tourmaline	Complex borosilicate	Trigonal	7½	3.06	1.62–1.64
Turquoise	Hydrated copper aluminium phosphate	Triclinic	6	2.80	1.61–1.65
Zircon	Zirconium silicate	Tetragonal	6½–7½	3.9–4.7	1.77–1.98

GLOSSARY OF GEM TERMS

ABSORPTION SPECTRUM
The pattern of dark lines seen when white light is examined under a special instrument, just after that light has passed through a gemstone. The dark bands appear because certain colours of the spectrum have been absorbed by the stone

AMORPHOUS
Lacking a regular structure or shape, that is, non-crystalline

ASTERISM
Star effect seen when some stones are cut as cabochons

BIREFRINGENCE
The difference between the largest and smallest Refractive Indexes of stones that are doubly refractive

BRILLIANT
A fine, many faceted diamond

CABOCHON
Gem that is cut and polished into a simple, domed shape. Such stones are often said to be cut *en cabochon*

CARAT (CT)
Unit used to measure the weight of gems; one carat equals one fifth of a gram. The purity of gold is also measured in carats and pure gold is 24 carat

CARBUNCLE
Any bright red gemstone with a cabochon cut

CHATOYANCY
An effect rather like a cat's eye, seen when a stone is cut as a cabochon

CLEAVAGE
Where a stone has fractured in a certain direction, due to weaknesses in the atomic structure

CROWN
The uppermost part of a cut stone

CRYPTOCRYSTALLINE
Where minerals are made up of tiny crystals, only visible through a microscope

CRYSTAL
Material with flat faces and a specific internal structure that dictates its external shape.

CUT
The way in which facets have been cut into a stone

DIFFRACTION
The way in which white light splits into the rainbow colours of the spectrum when it passes through a small hole

DISPERSION
The way in which white light splits into the rainbow colours of the spectrum when it passes through a stone. Also known as "fire"

DOUBLE REFRACTION (DR)
The way in which a ray of light entering a stone is refracted by different amounts

DOUBLET
Stone consisting of two pieces of material joined together artificially

FACE
Flat surface on the outside of a crystal

FACET
Flat surface of a cut, polished gemstone

FIRE *see* Dispersion

FRACTURE
Uneven breaking of a gem, unrelated to its internal structure

GEM
Any material valued for its beauty or rarity

GIRDLE
The widest part of a gemstone

HEAT TREATMENT
Heating stones in order to change the colour in some way

IGNEOUS ROCK
Rock formed from cooled lava or magma

INCLUSION
Anything found within a gemstone, such as crystals of another mineral, small gas- or liquid-filled spaces, or plant and animal matter. Some are visible with the naked eye; others only with a microscope

IRIDESCENCE
The way in which the internal structure of a stone splits white light into the colours of the spectrum, producing a play of rainbow hues

LAPIDARY
Someone who cuts and polishes gemstones

LAVA
The molten material that flows from a volcano and later cools to a solid

LUSTRE
How shiny the surface of a gem is, depending on the way light reflects off its surface

MAGMA
Fluid material from inside the Earth, which forms igneous rock when cool

MATRIX
The host rock in which gem material is found

METAMORPHIC ROCK
Rocks that originally had a different form, but were changed by intense heat and/or pressure

MICROCRYSTALLINE
Mineral material with such tiny crystals that they can only be seen under a miscroscope

MINERAL
Naturally occurring inorganic material with a fixed structure and composition

MIXED-CUT
Cut stone with a different pattern of facets above and below the stone's girdle

MOHS' SCALE
A standard scale used to measure the hardness of a stone, named after a German mineralogist called Friedrich Mohs. The scale runs from 1 to 10 and is based on how easily a stone can be scratched; at a given "rung" of this scale, a stone can scratch all those below it on the scale and will be scratched by all those above

OPALESCENCE
A kind of iridescence with a milky blue tinge

ORGANIC GEM
Any gem originally formed from living animal or plant matter

PASTE
Imitation gems made from glass

PAVILION
The bottom half of a cut stone, below the girdle

POLYCRYSTALLINE
Mineral matter made up of lots of small crystals

REFRACTION
The way in which natural white light is slowed down and bent as it passes from the air into a gemstone

REFRACTIVE INDEX (RI)
A scale for measuring the refraction of a certain stone

RHOMBIC
Shaped like a cube leaning to one side

ROUGH
The natural state of gem material, before it is cut or polished

SEDIMENTARY ROCK
Rock formed from a mix of substances – mineral fragments, plant matter and so on – that has collected as a sediment and hardened over time

SPECIFIC GRAVITY (SG)
A scale for measuring the density of a gem, based on how its weight compares with the weight of the same volume of water

STEP-CUT
A stone cut into a kind of lozenge shape with a series of rectangular facets, including a distinctive rectangular table facet above

TABLE
The central facet of a gem's crown

TRANSITION ELEMENTS
Elements that have entered mineral material while it is forming and give it its colour

INDEX

FURTHER READING

ANDERSON, B. W., *Gem Testing*, Butterworth, London

ARMSTRONG, Nancy, *Victorian Jewellery*, Studio Vista, London

BAKER, Margaret, *Folklore of the Sea*, David & Charles, London

BLACK, J. Anderson, *A History of Jewels*, Orbis. London

BRUTON, Eric, *Diamonds*, N.A.G. Press, London

CAVENDISH, R. (ed.), *Mythology*, W. H. Smith, London

COHANE, John. P., *The Key*, Turnstone Books, London

COLLINS, Wilkie, *The Moonstone*, published 1868

DESAUTELS, Paul. E., *The Gem Kingdom*, Ridge Press, New York

EVANS, Joan, *Magical Jewels of the Middle Ages*, Clarenden Press, Oxford

FERNIE, William. T., *The Occult and Curative Powers of Precious Stones*, R. Steiner, New York

GEM INSTITUTE OF AMERICA, *Diamond. Famous, Notable and Unique*, G.I. America, New York

GOLDIN, H.E. *Book of Legends*, Hebrew Pub. Co., New York

GUBELIN, Eduard, *Precious Stones*, Hallewag Ltd., Berne

HALL, Cally, *Eyewitness Handbook/Gemstones*, Dorling Kindersley, London and *Gems and Precious Stones*, The Apple Press, London

HEAPS, Willard, *Birthstones and the Lore of Gemstones*, Angus & Robertson, London

HOWES, Michael, *Amulets*, Robert Hale & Co. London

HUNGER, Rosa, *The Magic of Amber*, N.A.G. Press, London

JONES, William, *Precious Stones, Their History and Mystery*, R. Bently & Son, London

KOZMINSKY, Isadore, *The Magic and Science of Jewels and Stones*, Putnams & Sons, London

KUNZ, Geo F., *Rings for the Finger*, Dover Publications, New York

KUNZ, Geo F., *The Curious Lore of Precious Stones*, Dover Publications, New York

KUNZ Geo F., *The Magic of Jewels and Charms*, Lippincot, New York

LEACH, Maria (ed), *Dictionary of Folklore, Mythology and Legend*, Funk & Wagnalls, New York

LEGRAND, Jaques, *Diamond. Myth, Magic, Reality*, Crown Publishers, New York

MERCER, Ian, *Crystals*, Natural History Museum, London

O'DONOGHUE, Michael (ed), *Encyclopedia of Minerals and Gemstones*, Orbis Ltd, London

RADFORD, Edwin, *Encyclopedia of Superstitions*, Helicon, London

ROYAL NETHERLANDS ACADEMY, *The Shorter Encyclopedia of Islam*, Luzak & Co, London

SCHUMAN, Walter, *Gemstones of the World*, N.A.G. Press, London

SCOTT, Reginald, *Discoverie of Witchcraft*, published 1584

SHACKLEY, Myrna, *Rocks and Man*, Geo.Allen & Unwin, London

TURZAKER, James, *Gemstones and Their Occult Power*, Merlin Publications, London

THOMAS & PAVITT, *The Book of Talismans, Amulets and Zodiacal Gems*, Wilshire Book Company, Hollywood

TRUSTEES, BRITISH MUSEUM, *Jewellery Through 7,000 years*, British Museum Publications, London

WALKER, Barbara G., *The Book of Sacred Stones*, HarperCollins, San Francisco

WEBSTER, Robert, *Gems in Jewellery*, N.A.G. Press, London

WEBSTER, Robert, *Practical Gemmology*, N.A.G. Press, London

WHITLOCK, Ralph, *In Search of Ghosts*, David and Charles, London

ACKNOWLEDGEMENTS

The publishers would like to thank the following sources for their permission to reproduce the images in this book:

Ancient Art & Architecture Collection 11, 31, 147;

AKG London 108, 119, 123, 141, 142, 146;

Bridgeman Art Library 73, 112-3, 132, /Bonhams 56, 59 bottom, 64-5;

British Crown Copyright 20, 58, 88, 90;

Bruce Coleman 118, 124;

Christie's Colour Library 24, 27, 41 top, 42, 46, 89, 63, 148;

De Beers 82, 87, 90;

ET Archive 144 /Hist Mus Moscow 55, /Uffizi 64;

Fortean Picture Library 136;

Images Colour Library 10, 16, 25, 42 bottom, 49, 72, 77, 92, 116, 120 left, 138 top, 100;

Mansell Collection 144 left;

Mary Evans Picture Library 36, 40, 61, 65 right, 74, 80, /Explorer 84, 102, 108, 111, 112-3, 114, 116, 120, 121, 122, 126, 128, 150;

Natural History Museum 12, 20, 22, 23, 26, 28, 32, 38, 41 bottom, 44, 48, 52, 56, 57, 59 top, 66, 68-9, 70, 74, 75, 79, 80, 81, 82, 85, 86, 101, 104, 124, 132, 134 top & bottom, 135, 137, 139, 143, 156, 157;

Science Photo Library 94, 114, /Fleming 2 inset, 28, 67, 76, 98, 105, 106, /Fred K Smith 69, /George Chan 6, /Geospace 107, /Gugliemo 34, 35, 36, 78, /Hart-Davis 8, /Jisas /Lockheed 38, /John Walsh 1, 60, /Kage 136, /Kuylk 9, /Land 33, /Manfred Kage 50, /Martin Land 62, /Parker 18, 149, /Parviainen 96, /Pasieka 14, /Revy 18, /Stammers 2, 98, 102, /Stevenson 3 inset, /Tompkinson 145 right;

Werner Forman Archive/British Musem 45, 55 /Egyptian Museum 51.